MW01122137

HIGH LIFE

BROCKVILLE
DAVID SAVOY.
MAR. 10. 14 T.O.
GLL
PHONE# (519)252 8563

# HIGH LIFE

BY LEE MacDOUGALL

*High Life*
first published 1997 by
Scirocco Drama
An imprint of J. Gordon Shillingford Publishing Inc.
© 1996 Lee MacDougall

Scirocco Drama Editor: Dave Carley
Cover design by Terry Gallagher/Doowah Design
Author photo by Helen Tansey
Cover photo of Brent Carver and Randy Hughson by Wanda Goodwin
Printed and bound in Canada

Published with the generous assistance of The Canada Council

Canadian Cataloguing in Publication Data

MacDougall, Lee, 1957-
    High life

ISBN 1-896239-19-6

    I. Title.

PS8575.D6833H54 1997        C812'.54        C97-9900096-3
PR9199.3.M312H54 1997

*For Tim French*

# Acknowledgements

I would like to thank the many people who have given me encouragement, or been involved in the development of this play: Blake Heathcote, Tom Wood, Celia Chassels, Charles Northcote, Candace Burley and Iris Turcott of Canadian Stage Company's New Play Development Program, Jim Millan and Crow's Theatre, and all the very talented actors who have been involved in readings, workshops, or productions.

During the writing of this play, I was grateful to be the recipient of a grant from the Ontario Arts Council, and an award from the Tyrone Guthrie Awards Committee of the Stratford Festival (1995).

# Production History

The play was first read for the author in August, 1994, by Tom McCamus, Stephen Ouimette, Peter Donaldson, and Duncan Ollerenshaw. A reading/workshop of the play took place at Canadian Stage Company in March, 1995, with the following cast:

DICK ..................................................................... Ron White
BUG ................................................................ Daniel Kash
DONNIE ....................................................... Alan Williams
BILLY ............................................................. Martin Julien

A staged reading was presented at the Stratford Festival in September, 1995. It was directed by the author, stage managed by Henry Bertrand, stage directions read by Bradley C. Rudy, sound by Keith Handegord, and performed by:

DICK .............................................................. Tom McCamus
BUG ................................................................. David Keeley
DONNIE .................................................... Stephen Ouimette
BILLY .............................................................. Stuart Hughes

In April, 1996, *High Life* was presented by Crow's Theatre as part of the du Maurier World Stage Festival at Toronto's Harbourfront Centre. It was directed by Jim Millan, produced by Nancy McLeod and Jim Millan, stage managed by Mike Wallace, lighting design by Bonnie Beecher, design consultant Glenn Davidson, fight direction by John Stead, with the following cast:

DICK .................................................................. Ron White
BUG ............................................................ Randy Hughson
DONNIE ........................................................ Brent Carver
BILLY .......................................................... Clive Cholerton

The Crow's Theatre production of *High Life* received five Dora Mavor Moore nominations in 1996. The author won the Dora for Best New Play and the Dora for Best Actor went to Brent Carver.

Lee MacDougall

Actor Lee MacDougall has performed in theatres all across Canada. He has been a member of the Stratford Festival Company for five seasons, spent three seasons at the Shaw Festival, and appeared at the Royal Alexandra Theatre, the Elgin Theatre, the Citadel Theatre, the Charlottetown Festival, the National Arts Centre and Neptune Theatre, among others.

*High Life* is Lee's first play. As of publication he is working on a new play, and a screenplay.

# About the Play

In 1989 I worked at a regional theatre, and was billeted in a house with a few other boarders. The men in that house and their daily visitors were the inspiration for this play. Some of them were ex-convicts; all were addicted to morphine.

A morphine addict is nothing like the stereotypical model of a heroin addict presented in film and television. Morphine addiction takes its toll, but so does everyday life. Morphine is injected intramuscularly, as opposed to heroin which is injected intravenously, therefore morphine addicts can "fix" in any muscle large enough to receive a needle. The similarity is that the daily activities of an addict are focused on one thing, one bottom line: feeding the addiction.

These characters are from all over Canada, so attempts at a uniform regional dialect should be avoided. The piece plays best without an interval, but if you choose to insert one, the natural break occurs after Scene Four. Some of the dialogue is meant to overlap; the (/) denotes the point at which the next speaker should begin. The punctuation and line breaks are deliberate.

The names have been changed to protect me.

A brief glossary of addiction terms:

| | |
|---|---|
| jonesin' | in dire need of a fix |
| to cook | to mix the crushed pills with water, and boil off the impurities, prior to injection |

# Scene One

*(The play takes place in May 1989, in a Canadian city.*

*Much of the action takes place in the house where DICK is staying. It is a simple, middle-class dwelling, fairly neat, something a teacher might own. The space is open, kitchen stage right, and living room stage left. The entrance from outside is off the living room, there is a section of the stairs to the second floor visible between the two rooms, and various doors to other rooms off the kitchen.*

*DICK is a lean, intelligent man. He has been in and out of prisons since he was 17, he is now in his late 30's, but looks 40-something. BUG, real name Michael, has a similar history. He is a brutal man.*

*As the scene begins, we discover DICK and BUG in mid-conversation.)*

BUG:    *(Excitedly.)* and *then* Buddy gets out, eleven years, but not on the day he's supposed to, there was some fuck-up, anyway gets out, and flies home to what's-her-name—

DICK:   Who.

BUG:    Buddy Fingerote.

DICK:   No, her.

BUG:    Fuck I dunno, Rita or Ricky, somethin' like that, anyway gets home, breaks in—she's not there. All those letters, all those visits,

DICK:   All those tears,

| | |
|---|---|
| BUG: | Ya, so he freaks for a bit, figures she must be at her mum's er somethin', so he goes over to his buddy's place— |
| DICK: | Who. |
| BUG: | You don't know him. |
| DICK: | I know him. |
| BUG: | Beans Dohanik. |
| DICK: | O.K. I don't know him. |
| BUG: | Gets over to Beans's place, music playing real loud, door's unlocked, figures he's just partyin', lets himself in. *(He stands.)* Walks through the house, music poundin', no one around. Goes upstairs, maybe he's passed out, goes into the bedroom, there's Beans. In bed, doin' Buddy's wife! |
| DICK: | Whatsername! |
| BUG: | They don't see him! He loses it. Walks downstairs, gets one of Beans's rifles, a .404 I think, loads it, comes back up, music's still goin', they're still goin', stands at the foot of the bed, blows one right into Beans's back. |
| DICK: | He was on top. |
| BUG: | Bullet goes right through him, misses everything, and kills her. |
| DICK: | Betty? |
| BUG: | BRENDA! *(He sits.)* |
| | *(Beat.)* |
| | Kills her, and he lives. |
| DICK: | No way. |
| BUG: | Fuckin' right. |
| DICK: | How come I never heard about it? |
| BUG: | He was only out one day... |

DICK:      What he get?

BUG:       Eight to ten.

DICK:      For murder?

BUG:       It was an accident.
           Said he was just tryin' to scare them.

DICK:      Oh.

           *(Pause.)*

           You been home yet?

BUG:       Not in about twenty years.

DICK:      What? You mean you haven't seen yer Mom in all
           that time?

BUG:       No, I've seen her—she visited me in a couple of
           places.

DICK:      Prisons.

BUG:       Ya.

DICK:      Jesus. Go home. Go see your friends. That little shit-
           hole of a town deserves it.

BUG:       Really.

DICK:      *(Sings.)* Yes they'll all run to greet me... *(from
           "Green Green Grass of Home.")*

BUG:       *(Laughs.)* With fuckin' shotguns.

DICK:      Some of them, probably, yes. The ones that remem-
           ber you.

           *(Beat.)*

           So you wanna hear my thing?

BUG:       Your what?

DICK:      My thing.
           My plan I been workin' on.
           The Bank Thing!

| | |
|---|---|
| BUG: | Don't even bother. |
| DICK: | You don't wanna hear it? |
| BUG: | Don't talk to me. |
| DICK: | It's pretty good. |
| BUG: | Don't even fuckin' look at me. |
| DICK: | As a matter of fact, this one is perfect. "Failsafe", if you'll pardon the pun. |
| BUG: | What? |
| DICK: | Never mind. You wanna hear it? |
| BUG: | No. Shut up. I'm out one day. Fuck, one day. |
| DICK: | I waited for you. *(Beat.)* It's perfect. |
| BUG: | Ya, just like the last one. Me—seven years, you—fuck all. Or the one before, both of us, and Donnie, four a piece. / Or the... |
| DICK: | Don't blame any of your time on me. You're the asshole who killed that fuckin'...security guard. |
| BUG: | *(Sulking.)* I didn't kill him. |
| DICK: | *(Laughing.)* Oh, excuse me, he musta had a heart attack just as you hit him. |
| BUG: | Just because you hit someone and they die, doesn't mean you killed them. |
| DICK: | I'll have to think about that one. |
| BUG: | I shouldn't even be here. |
| DICK: | You're right. |
| BUG: | You're off fuckin' limits for my parole. |
| DICK: | I know. |
| BUG: | I can't be with you. |

*(Beat.)*

| | |
|---|---|
| DICK: | What took you so long? |
| BUG: | I couldn't find ya. |
| DICK: | I moved a few times. |
| BUG: | Whose place is this? |
| DICK: | Nice eh? My Rehab counsellor. |
| BUG: | He lets you/ |
| DICK: | I'm clean. |
| BUG: | Really. |
| DICK: | I am clean. |

*(Beat.)*

| | |
|---|---|
| BUG: | That's too bad. |
| DICK: | What've you got? |
| BUG: | Nothing. What about you? |
| DICK: | Ah Bug...you son of a gun. What you come here for? Advice? Counselling from a brother who has seen the light?... Or maybe just a little mind-fuck. |
| BUG: | What've you got? |
| DICK: | Some pink. Some grey. |
| BUG: | What do ya wanna do first? |
| DICK: | First? You're planning a party. |
| BUG: | Fuckin' right. |

*(DICK moves a chair to the counter, stands on it, reaches above the cupboards for a syringe.)*

| | |
|---|---|
| DICK: | There's spoons and stuff in there. *(Pointing to drawer.)* |
| BUG: | Me first. *(BUG gets two spoons.)* |
| DICK: | *(Back at the table, takes kleenex from shirt pocket, revealing pills.)* So you wanna hear my thing? |

BUG:          No.

DICK:         You sure?

BUG:          Just do it.

DICK:         Wanna cook?

BUG:          No...

DICK:         *(He begins to crush two pills with the spoons.)* Remember Joan?

BUG:          Fuck, she could cook.

DICK:         The best. Get some water. Yes...Joan, Joan, The Con-Hag.

BUG:          Ya... How is she?

DICK:         *(Thinks.)* ...Still dead.

BUG:          Fuck.

DICK:         No thanks.

BUG:          Really. She was sad lookin'. *(Beat.)* Who killed her?

DICK:         Tattoo.

BUG:          Fuckin' Tattoo. What for?

DICK:         She ripped him off. *(He mixes the crushed pills with some of the water in one of the spoons.)*

BUG:          No.

DICK:         He said.

BUG:          Where's he?

DICK:         Uh...dead. *(Heats mixture over a lighter.)*

BUG:          Fuck no eh?

DICK:         Oh ya.

BUG:          Dead?

DICK:         Real dead.

BUG:     Who did him?

DICK:    Hard Rock.

BUG:     Fuck.

DICK:    Blasted him good.

BUG:     Good. Where is he?

DICK:    Arse-Fuckin'-Wipe! *You* killed *Him*!

BUG:     Oh ya. *(Beat.)* I didn't like him.

DICK:    I hope not. Jesus…
         Remember him taking the rap for that boat job?

BUG:     What boat?

DICK:    Mahone's boat.

BUG:     *(Laughing.)* Oh ya…what happened to Mahone?

DICK:    The Klan got him.

BUG:     The Klan? Here?

DICK:    Yes here. Don't you remember us living in that fucking trailer, six months in the bush, hiding from the Klan?

BUG:     *(Thinks.)* …Why were they after us?

DICK:    Fucked if I know. *(Filling syringe.)*

BUG:     Somethin' about a girl…

DICK:    Ya, back then it was always about a girl. Or drugs. Or a girl on drugs…

BUG:     Hurry up.

DICK:    Don't fuckin' hurry me. It's ready. Where you want it?

BUG:     My leg. My arms are fucked.

DICK:    That's not all.

BUG:     What?

| | |
|---|---|
| DICK: | So are mine. How long has it been? |
| BUG: | About eight. |
| DICK: | This morning? |
| BUG: | Last night. |
| DICK: | Oh Bugboy, you got it bad. |
| BUG: | Fuckin' right. *(Rolls up pants, leg is badly scarred. He puts his foot on the coffee table.)* |
| DICK: | *(Holding needle away.)* You'll listen to my plan? |
| BUG: | Do it. |
| DICK: | You're gonna love it. |
| BUG: | Don't start. DON'T FUCKIN' START WITH ME. |
| DICK: | Are you sure? |
| BUG: | I'll kill you. |
| DICK: | You wouldn't do that... |
| BUG: | Do me. Then / |
| DICK: | Then what? |
| BUG: | Then you. |
| DICK: | Bug... |
| BUG: | THEN TELL ME. |
| DICK: | That's my Bugboy. *(Tapping air bubbles out of syringe.)* |

*(BUG closes eyes, holds breath.)*

Bug. Your leg. Gross. *(Injects calf.)*

| | |
|---|---|
| BUG: | *(Exhales.)* Fuck you, Dickie. *(Rolls down pant leg, paces, scratching scalp.)* Yes. Yes. |

*(Heartbeat sound in faintly.)*

DICK:     Come here. *(Removes shoe and sock, foot is scarred.)*

BUG:      Fuck you.

DICK:     Maybe later. *(Another joke.)*

BUG:      What?

DICK:     Come here. Here. *(Holding foot up.)*

BUG:      Your foot? *(Heartbeat louder.)*

DICK:     What was your first clue?

BUG:      Fuck. *(Sits, takes syringe.)* Do it yourself.

DICK:     Just fuckin' do it. God knows you've done it in worse places.

          *(Heartbeat building.)*

BUG:      Remember Deadeye? Taking it out / and having to do him right into his—

DICK:     DON'T TALK TO ME ABOUT THAT FUCKER. *(BUG stabs needle into the arch of DICK's foot. DICK screams.)*

          *(Beat.)* Thank you.

          *(The heartbeat fades to silence.)*

BUG:      Fuck you. *(Throws the needle in the sink.)*

          *(Pause during which DICK pulls his sock up, puts his shoe back on. BUG sits at the kitchen table.)*

BUG:      Where'd you get this?

          *(Beat.)*

          Dick?

          *(Beat.)*

          Dickless?

DICK:     Huh?

BUG:      Where'd you get this?

| DICK: | *(Thinks.)* Corpse. |
|---|---|
| BUG: | What? |
| DICK: | Corpse. |
| BUG: | What corpse? |
| DICK: | Fuck you have been away. Corpse is a friend of Donnie's, they met in the hospital, he's got cancer, and he shares his...wealth. |
| BUG: | He sells his medication? |
| DICK: | Cheap. |
| BUG: | Beautiful. *(Beat.)* Why do you call him Corpse? |
| DICK: | He looks like he died about four years ago. |
| BUG: | Shit. |
| DICK: | Weighs about seventy pounds. |
| BUG: | *(Laughs.)* What's he do with the money? |
| DICK: | WELL HE'S NOT BUYING FUCKIN' FOOD! |

*(Both laugh. Beat.)*

| BUG: | How is Donnie? |
|---|---|
| DICK: | Alive. |
| BUG: | Fuck. |
| DICK: | Just. |
| BUG: | Fuckin' Donnie. |
| DICK: | Yes fuckin' Donnie. I like Donnie. I don't know why, but I think he serves some purpose. He's still on morphine, it's still killing him, his kidneys are a cunt-hair from collapsing completely, he looks like shit, he whines worse than ever—but he's still the best thief I ever met. |
| BUG: | I hate Donnie. |

DICK: You don't understand him. Donnie is a pure criminal. Behind that pale, pathetic exterior lies the mind of a genius. A genius with no guilt. He has no conscience. And he invents crime. It just comes to him. He has this beautiful thing going now with bank machines.

BUG: Bank machines?

DICK: I'll tell you later. But it is Donnie, and his beautiful thing, that is the opening of my…idea.

BUG: No way. No fuckin' way. Nothin' with Donnie. No way I'm touchin' anything with that… Not again. He's dyin'. He's fuckin' dyin'—an' he's bad luck.

DICK: We're all dying Fuck. Donnie just likes to talk about it. All the time. And this plan is so Foolproof, that neither he or you or Billy or any asshole's bad luck could ever fuck it up.

BUG: Who's Billy?

DICK: Billy is new. *(He lights a cigarette.)* He's…different. Very clean. I met him at a Narcotics Anonymous meeting.

BUG: What the fuck?

DICK: Drug Rehab. You go, people talk about shit, you connect later, you make deals.

BUG: This guy is on morphine?

DICK: Yes Bug, he is a raving morphadite.

BUG: A what?

DICK: Like you and me, but not exactly. He's a charmer. But kind of cocky. Good looking. Very clean-like. He has this thing going with nurses; he dates them, etc., and they get it for him…he says he needs it for his mother.

BUG: *(Beat.)* I don't like him.

DICK: I'll allow that. *(Getting beer from the fridge.)* He hasn't shown up yet. But he will. He'll come. And when he does, you keep your eye on him. 'Cause we need him. And we need Donnie, and we need you, *(Giving BUG a beer.)* and you need me. For my perfect plan.

BUG:         Not me.

DICK:        Oh yes. You, Bug-twat. You see, I feel I owe you this one. Having spent most of our lives inside, we deserve this. I'm talking major money. Easy major money.

BUG:         No fuckin' way.

DICK:        Enough for you to buy that ranch. Those horses. You could do it, Bug. This time. Up in the mountains, riding those babies, breaking them, breeding them, whatever you want to do. You could get there…for good.

               *(Pause.)*

               *(BUG finally looks at him.)*

               THAT'S MY BUGBOY NOW YOU FUCKIN' LISTEN TO ME AND YOU LISTEN GOOD.

               *(He slaps BUG's face.)*

               O.K., this is it.

               *(Beat. Blackout. Music in.)*

# Scene Two

*(The next day, the same house. DICK and DONNIE are seated in the kitchen.)*

DONNIE: So I'm in the emergency ward there eh? and this doctor, real young asshole, says how old are you—he's looking at me like this is it—like I'm gonna kick right in front of him—so he goes how old are you, like he can't believe that I could have all these things wrong with me and be under fifty, but he knows I can't be that old, 'cause I don't look that bad—so he's totally fucked up, an' he's startin' to sweat a bit eh, an' he's an' he's shakin'? An' I say twenty-nine. An' he just goes pale, like white eh? sort of blue-white? An' I thought this nurse and I were gonna have to give him C.P. fuckin' R. or somethin'. Then this nurse—real old hard babe eh? yellow hair, and teeth, she's been up there for years, she's knows what's goin' on—she says "Oh Donald has lived long and hard those twenty-nine years Doctor"—and I grabs my thing an' I goes "Oh Winnie, that was supposed to be our little secret!"

*(Laughs hard, which becomes hard coughing, which subsides when he lights a cigarette.)*

DICK: So how are ya?

DONNIE: Well my one kidney is completely fucked—like dead—and the other one is only working at like forty percent or somethin', but they can't do the operation 'cause they can't find me a good match—but I'm on the waiting list—an' also 'cause my heart is so fucked up, and my pressure is all over the place, but my lungs are a bit better, they said that pneumonia I had is almost gone / and my stomach

| | |
|---|---|
| DICK: | But you feel…all right? |
| DONNIE: | Oh ya, ya—I only get sick when I eat—an' I'm not throwin' up every time now. *(Beat.)* They don't know what it is. |
| DICK: | But you're strong enough to |
| DONNIE: | Oh ya, I get around. And stuff. |
| DICK: | That's good. Still got that thing going with the bank machines? |

*(Beat.)*

| | |
|---|---|
| DONNIE: | And what was that? |
| DICK: | You told me about it Donnie… Remember? |

*(Beat.)*

| | |
|---|---|
| DONNIE: | Oh ya that, I guess I did eh. Well ya, I still uh, ya you know…get around. |
| DICK: | You know I think you're brilliant Donnie. |
| DONNIE: | Oh you're just sayin' that can I have an ashtray? |
| DICK: | Sure. *(He pushes one to him.)* You want some of this? *(Bringing out syringe.)* |
| DONNIE: | Oh no—NO WAY—*(Moves away.)* I can't be doin' that shit—no fuck—no, not with my kidneys, or kidney, fuck, they told me at the clinic I would kill myself—fuckin' buy the farm if I ever do that again—ever—even one more time…no thank you—any time—that could be the one, the Last one. *(Beat.)* Nope. |
| DICK: | You're sure now. |
| DONNIE: | Oh ya, I'm sure. I'm off o' that stuff—that shit— right off. No Way. Not for me. |
| DICK: | But you don't mind if I do. |
| DONNIE: | Oh no, no you you go ahead—shit I don't mind— *(He moves back.)* jeez I'll help ya…um, no, I don't care. |

DICK:        Good. *(Places needle between them on coffee table.)*
             So give me the juice on your thing. Your bank
             machine thing. How do you do it?

DONNIE:      *(Beat.)* Well... It's fuck-all really. I just—I just fluked
             on that one. It's nothin'—I just uh...borrow
             people's wallets for a while, and I, and then, go to
             one of those machines, and withdraw a bit, uh,
             some... *(Shrugs.)* money.

DICK:        And then put the wallets back.

DONNIE:      Oh ya, if I can. Ya I always try to give 'em back their
             wallets and stuff 'cause that's...that's fuckin' awful
             when you lose all your I.D. an' that eh? that's such
             a pain, so whenever I—it takes forever to get all
             new cards again—so I always—if I can—get those
             back to them. Oh ya.

DICK:        How do you get the money?

DONNIE:      Well jeez at first that was hard—I had to run around
             from bank to bank depending on which cards they
             had, and it was killing me, all that running eh? took
             forever. But now, thank God, they got that Interac
             thing, where you can use any card at one machine,
             and fuck me it's so beautiful, now I can just go up to
             any one of them, and use all the cards. Fuck ya.

DICK:        No but how do you get the cash? Don't you need
             some code number or something?

DONNIE:      Ya.

DICK:        Well. How do you get the fuckin' numbers?

             *(Beat.)*

DONNIE:      Most people carry them in their wallets.

DICK:        The cards?

DONNIE:      The cards—*and* the numbers. They usually hide
             them in there real good, so ya really gotta look...but
             they're there.

DICK:        How many? What percentage?

DONNIE:     *(Thinks.)* Eighty.

DICK:     Beautiful.

DONNIE:     But I don't take much. Most of them probably don't even notice.

DICK:     Where do you get the wallets?

DONNIE:     Purses—usually.

DICK:     Where do you find the purses?

DONNIE:     Offices. Hospitals. Churches.

DICK:     Churches?

DONNIE:     But I put the wallets right back, an' I only take a bit from each one—an' I bet that most of 'em don't even know I was there.

> *(Beat.)*

Oh ya I can walk into a church, and they're in there cookin' or somethin' eh, an' they're afraid of someone stealin' their purses—an' I would be too—so they put them all in one room. So in ten minutes I'm in, out, and back. They don't know. They prob'ly don't even notice.

DICK:     And you don't feel bad about that? Those women?

DONNIE:     Nope. Should I?

DICK:     I guess not.

DONNIE:     I mean it's not like they're getting mugged or somethin'. Or someone grabbin' their purses and knockin' them down—that's fuckin' gross—I don't like that. This way they don't even notice, an' if they do, the bank tells them it was done with their card...which they still got.

DICK:     Perfect.

DONNIE:     Well...

> *(Beat. DICK picks up syringe.)*

DICK:         So you want to hear about my thing?

DONNIE:       Your thing.

DICK:         Ya, my idea. My plan. Almost as good as yours.

DONNIE:       I dunno...

DICK:         But bigger. Much bigger. One shot—one hit—Big. Very big money.

DONNIE:       Big?

DICK:         Huge. Gi-fuckin'-gantic. Enough for you, and me, and a few other guys to retire for a long, long time— very rich.

DONNIE:       Retire?

DICK:         Rich.

DONNIE:       Rich...

DICK:         Rich enough for you to buy anything Donnie. Anything. Need a kidney? You go anywhere you need to, and buy it. Or a heart. Or lungs, or anything you fuckin' well want.

DONNIE:       Buy it?

DICK:         Cash.

              *(Beat.)*

DONNIE:       What other guys?

DICK:         Ah Donnie you don't miss a trick do ya? Well one is a new guy, you don't know him, a very new guy, very clean, 's name is Billy.

DONNIE:       Uh huh.

DICK:         And the other guy you do know—from a long time ago—who is back, and better, and—well, fuck...it's Bug.

DONNIE:       *(Jumping up, pacing.)* NO WAY DICKIE, No way I can be—no way not Bug—Dick he will—no way I'm out of this fuckin' place—No Bug no Bug he is after me. He doesn't like me, and I don' like him and he scares / the shit—Dick he will

DICK:       Donnie. Donnie. He won't touch you. I'll see to it.

DONNIE:     No

DICK:       He will not touch you. We need him Donnie. We need him to...we just need him.

DONNIE:     No way.

DICK:       Hey! I need Bug to watch Billy.

DONNIE:     What—I thought you said

DICK:       Well, there's just something...I'm a little...Bug is my security—our security.

DONNIE:     I don't know.

DICK:       I'll protect you Donnie. He listens to me. You know that. He won't touch you.

            *(Beat.)*

            Remember me saving you from that big guy—the fat one? What was his name?

DONNIE:     Big Mac.

DICK:       Big Fuckin' Mackie, he was one scary lookin' mother—Jesus—and he liked you Donnie, from the word go, he wanted you bad, dead or alive.

DONNIE:     Eeyuhhh. *(He shudders in disgust.)*

DICK:       But I saved you, remember? He had you in the big kitchen, alone, and when I came in you were about two minutes from somethin' real nasty.

DONNIE:     Don't talk about it—he was so gross—
            *(Laughs.)* You stabbed him in the nuts!

DICK:       Ya... But I'll tell ya a secret. I know that kind of made me famous in there, being called the Nutcutter—but ya know what? I only meant to get him in that fat gut of his—but he was tall...I didn't aim high enough.

| | |
|---|---|
| DONNIE: | No way! |
| DICK: | Ya—I think I closed my eyes! It was an accident— well not really—I mean I meant to cut him, but not in the balls—that was just luck. *(Beat.)* He stayed away from you after that, didn't he? Stayed away from everybody. But I helped you, Donnie, I protected you from that Fat Fuck—and I can keep Bug away too...you know it. |

*(Beat.)*

Eh?

*(Beat.)*

| | |
|---|---|
| DONNIE: | Well... |
| DICK: | That's a boy! *(He moves beside him.)* |
| DONNIE: | What do you need me for? |
| DICK: | I need you baby for your perfect beautiful mind. And your bank machine thing. You do your purses—cards—bank machine number, and get us some money—just a bit—and then with that money, that little bit—we invest it, we use it to open the door to the big money—the big ticket—the Lottery big. Shopping for Organs big. "Kidneys are Us" big. |

*(Beat.)*

You want some? *(Indicating syringe.)*

| | |
|---|---|
| DONNIE: | You know I can't do that any more... |
| DICK: | Who told you that? |
| DONNIE: | That doctor at the clinic, and one of the nurses, and that guy at the / |
| DICK: | O.K. O.K. Do you believe them? |
| DONNIE: | Well...I don' know. |
| DICK: | Have you done any, since they told you this shit? |
| DONNIE: | ...A bit. |

DICK:        And have you croaked?

DONNIE:     *(Laughing.)* Not yet.

DICK:        So are they fucking liars?

DONNIE:     Maybe…

DICK:        Then you want some of this or not?

             *(Beat.)*

DONNIE:     Let's have some of mine. *(Throws a pill bottle full of greys to DICK.)*

DICK:        *(Seeing number of pills.)* Fuck Donnie! Roxanol!

DONNIE:     A lucky purse. I need them more than she does. They're not good for her.

DICK:        You want one?

DONNIE:     …One can't hurt.

DICK:        That's a boy. Jesus baby, you had me scared for a minute there. Don't you go gettin' all religious on me, listening to people who don't know dick about shit. Those medical types, they know we've tapped into something amazing here, and they don't know what it is, they just know if it's that good, it's gotta be bad for you. Gotta kill you.
             They're like Baptists. You keep away from them. Just run the other way. Satan get behind me.

             *(Beat.)*

             You're not dying.
             Now…you wanna hear my thing?

             *(Pause. DONNIE smiles.)*

DONNIE:     O.K. Dick.

             *(Blackout. Music.)*

# Scene Three

*(DICK and BILLY. DICK is cleaning up the kitchen, BILLY is seated in the living room.)*

BILLY: And so I ended up here finally, to get away from the heroin. I hustled for a while when I was a kid, got into horse—too soon—but that can happen. But the stuff you get now is full of who knows what kind of shit—and then you get some that's so pure it kills you. At least with morphine you know what you're getting, and it's easier to come by. So I came out here because there's not a lot of horse around…and…I had some lady friends who were starting to ask some questions. *(DICK looks at him at the mention of women.)*

DICK: How many? *(Moving into living room.)*

BILLY: Pardon me?

DICK: How many women were you screwing?

BILLY: …I have a fondness for the ladies.

DICK: At one time, in one week, how many would you be fond of?

BILLY: Roughly…ten.

DICK: That's two a day.

BILLY: Sometimes three.

> *(Beat.)*

I love women.

DICK: You love fucking.

BILLY:      Women.

            *(Pause. Then DICK sits.)*

DICK:       And how did you find me?

BILLY:      I followed one of your friends.

DICK:       Who?

BILLY:      A big guy with... *(Points to a tattoo on his hand.)*

DICK:       Bug.

BILLY:      Bug. *(Beat.)* We met in a bar. I can tell a user when I see one. He was easy. We talked, I followed him. I like to deal direct.

DICK:       Bug wouldn't like to know he was followed.

BILLY:      He won't. *(Beat.)* I'm not afraid of Bug.

DICK:       You're not.

BILLY:      No. He's not smart enough.

            *(Beat.)*

DICK:       He is. And you should be. Be very afraid of Bug. Be careful.

BILLY:      I am.

            *(Beat.)*

DICK:       You've never been inside, have you?

BILLY:      I can't say as I've had the pleasure.

DICK:       It shows.

BILLY:      Oh?

DICK:       You look young. Unscarred. You have all your teeth.

            *(BILLY smiles.)*

            I can see why the ladies go for you.

BILLY:     Are you coming on to me?

DICK:      Do you want me to?... *(Beat.)* No Billy, I didn't let you in to play with you.

        *(DICK lights a cigarette.)*

        I saw you at the Narcotics Anonymous meeting, about a week ago—you were very good. But I'm like you, I can smell a user a long way off. I knew you'd come.

BILLY:     Here I am.

DICK:      And here you are...

        *(Beat.)*

        What's the one thing you need, right now—more than anything—that would solve all your problems, and make everything...right.

BILLY:     Morphine.

DICK:      And if I could give you all the morphine you'd ever need in your life, forever, what would you want then?

BILLY:     *(Thinks.)* ...Morphine.

DICK:      O.K....just checking. Before we do our "business", I'd like to talk to you about an idea of mine.

BILLY:     What kind of idea.

DICK:      A job. Ever done a job before?

BILLY:     Several.

DICK:      And you've never done time.

BILLY:     I don't get caught.

DICK:      I marvel at you.

        *(Beat.)*

        What I'd like to talk to you about, involves some

very big money, and a bank—and no one wants to get caught with bank money.

BILLY:  No.

DICK:  No, because for some strange reason known only to the powers that be, and one that says a lot about how fucked up things are these days, you do more time for robbing a bank than for murder. Banks are very well protected, they make billions every year, they don't pay any taxes—

BILLY:  But you have an idea.

DICK:  *(Beat.)* Yes I do.

*(Beat.)*

BILLY:  Why do you want me?

DICK:  Well...you came to me. And that tells me that I have something you need. And because of that need, I can guess that you go through a lot of money.

*(BILLY does not react.)*

And I can tell from the little games you've been playing with me—no, don't be offended, I've been around way too long, I've seen them all...I can tell how you get your stuff. You play a mean sex game, don't you. And the reason you're playin' with sex, is so you can keep bangin' up—I know that game. You move in on a woman—I think you said nurses—good line to good stuff—and give her a great story, and something else, and sweep her off her feet. And things go great for a while, don't they, but pretty soon, she wants more—and there's the problem. 'Cause all you want is morphine. And things get a little scary, especially if you've got a few going at once, and you do, and probably a few guys too eh? Don't bother. There's no such thing as a gay addict, or a straight one for that matter. I know, remember? You're just an addict. Which means you'll do anything for the shit. And I would too, if I looked like you.

But the problem is that when these things go sour,

you gotta move on, and on, and on, and pretty soon you're kind of runnin' aren't you. And sometimes it's hard to find people who haven't heard your story, and so you end up stuck—alone—without connections—and that brings you to me. So I know you Billy, and I know all the rules to all the games. And I know that if things were as easy and smooth for you as you'd like people to believe, you wouldn't be sitting here right now...waiting.

(Beat.)

We play a different game. Not being as lucky as you, we play the money game. Buying and selling. And to get our money, and to make life interesting, we play the Bandito game... It's fun.
And, right now, 'cause you need some money, I'm wondering if you wanna play with us for a bit. 'Cause if my idea works, you'll come out of it with a lot of money. More than you've ever made before.

BILLY: That's a lot...

DICK: Good.
You see, my game—involves someone who looks like you. Normal. Better than normal, which is a bonus. I need someone who can walk into a bank, and talk to a woman—and not cause a stir. Except maybe for her. If I, or any of my friends walk in— looking as we do—having lived our—difficult lives, every panic button in the place goes off, and the shit hits the fan. But if you go in, looking so

BILLY: Normal.

DICK: Healthy, if you walk up to a young lady, and talk with her, and bring something to her attention...she doesn't suspect a thing. She may even be distracted by your...way, your ability,

BILLY: and she gives me the money.

DICK: No...you give her the money.

BILLY: How do I

DICK: I'll explain all that later. (Brings out syringe.)

Are you in?

*(Beat.)*

BILLY:      I might could be persuaded.

DICK:       Good. *(Puts away syringe.)*
*(Rising, moving away.)* I want you to come back tomorrow.

BILLY:      Tomorrow?

DICK:       Ya.

BILLY:      *(Rising.)* But I'd really like to—I think I need to

DICK:       I really think I need you to come back tomorrow.

BILLY:      What for?

DICK:       To meet some friends of mine, talk this over.

BILLY:      Oh sure, ya, I can come back to meet—they're gonna be involved in—

DICK:       Ya, there are four of us. I need four.

BILLY:      No problem Dick. I can be here whenever you like.

DICK:       Good.

*(Beat.)*

So I'll see you then.

BILLY:      What time?

DICK:       Seven.

BILLY:      O.K...

DICK:       O.K... Goodbye.

*(Beat.)*

*(BILLY turns away, then back.)*

BILLY:      There was that other matter.

DICK:       There was?

BILLY:      The uh...business?

DICK:       Oh ya. You didn't think I'd forgotten, did you?

BILLY:      You had me worried.

DICK:       Good... I'll take care of you Billy.

*(Blackout. Music.)*

## Scene Four

*(The same rooms, 7:30 the following evening. DICK, DONNIE and BILLY are talking.)*

DONNIE: *(Flying.)* Oh ya, Dick was like a king, or a god inside. He was like Elvis.

DICK: Hardly.

DONNIE: No no, he was. My second time in?—my second bit?—when I got transferred to the big place, they called it Dick's Place—he fuckin' ran the joint. He had it all under control.

DICK: I had a few friends.

DONNIE: A few! You had everybody. He used to fly me a kite

BILLY: A what?

DONNIE: Oh—send me a message, through a screw... A pig—A dog!

DICK: He means a guard.

DONNIE: Ya! The fuckin' guards were like honoured to do things for him. 'Cause he had so much influence on what went down, and who did what—and by the time he got parole—by that time he was known as "the Warden".

BILLY: Really.

DONNIE: Oh fuck ya. They used to have these movie nights eh, where everybody once a week—well, not everybody, but most of us—we'd get together an' watch movies. Well it was Dick's idea—

DICK: It was not my fuckin' idea—

DONNIE:     I always thought you had...anyway they let him
            pick the movies 'cause he knows everything in the
            whole fuckin' history of movies ever, and so Dick
            got to pick which movie, or movies, 'cause there
            was usually two, and we saw some amazing

DICK:       People made suggestions, or asked for ones they
            liked—

DONNIE:     But you never played them!

DICK:       *(To BILLY.)* You can only see *Bird Man of Alcatraz* so
            many times.

BILLY:      Really.

DONNIE:     So he'd play the weirdest fuckin' movies ever eh?
            an' at first the guys were pissed off, but then they all
            started comin', 'cause, oh man, for a while he used
            to only show ones about women in prison, like
            *Women Behind Bars*! but really bad ones—

DICK:       Are there good ones?

DONNIE:     And Dick knows every person in every movie, like
            all their names and who directed it, an' oh,
            'member that French one—

BILLY:      French!

DONNIE:     Oh fuck ya, he had us watching really bizarre
            fuckin' every-language-in-the-world movies. What
            was that one French one Dick, about the guy, the
            guy who goes nuts, and starts to dress like a girl,
            and then throws himself out the window,
            *(Laughing.)* TWICE!

DICK:       *The Tenant.* Roman Polanski.

DONNIE:     *The Tenant*! Ya that was it, fuck that was weird.
            Almost started a riot that night, people were so
            fucked up by it. But I liked it. *(Beat.)*
            I didn't get it, but I liked it.

DICK:       With Shelley Winters as the concierge.

DONNIE:     See what I mean, he knows every person.

BILLY:          How did you get to know all these movies?

DICK:           Had about twenty years of free time on my hands…

DONNIE:         I liked that one.

BILLY:          I didn't realize movies were so big inside.

DICK:           Nothin' else to do.

DONNIE:         Didn't they show any where you did your time?

DICK:           Ah…

BILLY:          Pardon me?

DICK:           …Billy has—

DONNIE:         Where'd you do your time?

BILLY:          I've never done time.

                *(Beat.)*

DONNIE:         Never.

BILLY:          Nope.

                *(Pause.)*

DONNIE:         *(Rising.)* Uh maybe I'm just gonna go out and uh, /
                see what's— *(Moving towards door.)*

DICK:           Donnie—he is O.K. He has assured me he has been
                involved in many jobs before.

BILLY:          Many.

DICK:           Many escapades with the law, and has just been—
                well—unlucky so far, in that he hasn't been allowed
                to sample, to savour the hospitality of our various
                government hotels.

DONNIE:         That's too bad. He would have been popular.

DICK:           Yes… Billy has missed many of life's pleasures.

BILLY:          Not that many.

DICK:           Ooh…a colourful past.

| | |
|---|---|
| BILLY: | I've been around. |
| DICK: | He has also been around hospitals Donnie, something else you have in common. |
| DONNIE: | Are you sick? *(Moving away.)* |
| BILLY: | No. I just like to—I have a lot of friends who are in healthcare. |
| DONNIE: | Oh ya he told me you have this thing going with nurses getting you stuff. |
| BILLY: | Sometimes my friends will…help me out. |
| DICK: | Donnie likes to spend a lot of his time in hospitals. All of it. |
| DONNIE: | I have a couple of problems with my kidneys, and well, one of them is dead, and the other one is fucked, so I'm waiting for a transplant. *(Beat.)* I was born that way. |
| DICK: | Yes! After about twenty years of chemical abuse. |
| DONNIE: | I've always had |
| DICK: | You are so fucking full of drugs you glow in the dark! And how do you explain the bad liver, bad heart, lungs, stomach, blood, etc., etc.? Inbreeding? Between time inside, and time in hospitals, you've never cooked a hot meal in your life. |
| BILLY: | Eating all that hospital shit, it's no wonder you're sick. |
| DONNIE: | Exactly. |
| | *(Beat.)* |
| DICK: | Oh ya, our Donnie's had some real close calls in the medical world… |
| DONNIE: | What. |
| DICK: | You know…Doctor? |
| DONNIE: | Oh fuck. Oh ya. Long time ago, shit about eight or |

ten years eh? we used to follow doctors' cars aroun'—most of them don't do nothin', they just drive aroun'—anyway we'd cruise aroun' all day followin' them, waitin' for 'em to run into a store or somethin'—an' then we'd snag their medical bag.

DICK:          Bingo!

DONNIE:        Oh full of all kinds of shit.

DICK:          Then Bug and I got the idea to actually go undercover into the hospitals, and get into the pharmacies somehow, and clean them out. So we go in one day—we'd planned this for weeks—both of us looking like absolute shit as usual, long hair, not shaved—anyway we go in, and we find this bag of dirty laundry, we put on these orderly outfits, and start pushing around this stretcher—Christ I can't believe it—pretending we're taking it somewhere, and looking for the big stash. So we're freaking out—we both of us need it real bad—Bug's fuckin' shaking, and everybody's staring at us 'cause we look like a couple of carnival types, and we come around this corner real fast, and

DONNIE:        Fuckin' flyin' around the corner!

DICK:          We come whippin' around the corner, and knock down this doctor! Fuckin' take him right out—flat. So we grab the guy, and help him up

DONNIE:        And it's me!

DICK:          Fucking Donnie! Dressed up as a doctor. Lab coat, stethoscope, everything! Pulling the same scam we are.

DONNIE:        *(Rises.)* I didn't know you were—

DICK:          On the same day! Same hospital! And he looks about twelve years old.

DONNIE:        Oh man, I had people calling me—Doctor! Doctor!—all over the place—people fuckin' chasing me! I was runnin' terrified! Then OOOMPH! *(Imitates action of taking a stretcher in the stomach, falls to the couch laughing, which turns to coughing.)*

*(BUG enters from outside, moves quickly to DONNIE, grabs him by the shirt, backhands him hard across the face. DONNIE screams.)*

DICK:       Bug! No.

            *(BUG draws his arm back to punch DONNIE.)*

DICK:       Bug! This is Billy. *(Who has remained seated.)*

            *(BUG stops, looks at BILLY.)*

BILLY:      Hello Bug. *(Stays sitting.)*

BUG:        Fuck you.

            *(Beat.)*

DICK:       He likes you.

BILLY:      Likes me?

DICK:       You're still alive.

BUG:        And fuck you too. *(To DICK. He lowers his arm.)*

DICK:       Bugboy, why are you so filled with animal rage? And why have you hit Donnie?

BUG:        Fucker stole my tapes. *(Still standing over DONNIE.)*

DONNIE:     *(Crying.)* I never stole

            *(BUG goes to hit him again.)*

DICK:       Bug. Please. What tapes.

BUG:        *Born to Run.* And other stuff.

DICK:       When.

BUG:        Inside.

DICK:       That would have been what...1984? You mean to tell us that because you believe Donnie stole your tapes

DONNIE:     Never did

DICK:       Stole some very good music of yours, all those

|        | years ago, because of that suspicion, you are still harbouring all this hostility in your system? |
|--------|--------|
| BUG:   | What? |
| DICK:  | For that you want to kill him? |
| BUG:   | If I wanted to kill him he'd be dead. |
| DICK:  | Billy—I'd like you to meet "the Bug". |
| BILLY: | I believe we've met. |
| DICK:  | This is the new friend I told you about. He's going to help us. We are all going to help each other. Bug, why don't you go get yourself a beer. Please. |

*(Beat. BUG moves to kitchen.)*

| DONNIE: | I'm fuckin' gettin' the fuck outa here—you fuckers are crazy—you said you wouldn't let him, an' look, look at look at him fuckin' just comin' in here and beatin' on me. / I'm goin'—I don't need this shit. |
|---------|--------|
| DICK:   | *(Rises.)* Donnie. Stop. You are O.K. I need you to stay, please. I need you to help me. Hey—did you take his tapes? |
| DONNIE: | *(Crying.)* No. |
| DICK:   | Bug. He says it wasn't him who took your *Born to Run*. |
| BUG:    | *(Snorts.)* Who the fuck else would it have been. |
| DICK:   | IN A PRISON? I can think of a few. |

*(BILLY laughs, DONNIE smiles.)*

*(To BUG, quietly.)*

Hey, leave him alone. He's not feeling good

| BUG:  | Fuck. |
|-------|-------|
| DICK: | and we need him. Just like we need you, and Billy. Get a beer. Get me one too, and come and sit down. *(To DONNIE.)* Please stay. |

Everybody sit down. This is gonna be very good. Very easy. Very Big.

*(They move and settle, DONNIE ends up between BILLY and BUG on the couch.)*

DICK: Now I guess you're all wondering why I've called you here. *(Laughs.)*
As disciples of the evil Morph, we all go through a lot of money. We have an expensive hobby. We spend most of our time either getting stuff, or getting money for stuff. Now, what I have come up with, is a way for us to acquire some very heavy coin. A lot. For each of us.

DONNIE: I don't know.

DICK: Donnie, I like you…I'll kill you last.
I've told parts of this to a few of you, but now I'm gonna give you the whole Shebang. *(Thinks.)*
Donnie has this fucking brilliant thing worked out with bank machines. He takes peoples' wallets

DONNIE: Borrows

DICK: borrows their wallets, and goes to a bank machine, and withdraws money from their accounts.

BILLY/BUG: *(Together.)* How? / What?

DICK: Well, it seems that most people carry their code numbers with them. It is a beautiful scam, and he lives on it—he should be knighted for it—and it gave me an idea that is gonna make us all very happy.

BUG: *This* is your idea?

DICK: No. Listen. *(To DONNIE.)* How much money can you take out of one of those machines?

DONNIE: Oh uh well usually it's about 400—a day—but some of them are 5, and some are 8—it depends on the bank.

DICK: And how many people would you say go up to one, on any given day?

DONNIE:     Gee I dunno uh...hundreds, I guess. The busy ones.

DICK:       I guess hundreds too. And if each person can take out 5 or 8 hundred bucks...how much do you think is in each machine?

DONNIE:     Thousands...

BILLY:      Hundreds of thousands...

BUG:        Maybe.

DICK:       Ya maybe. But I want bigger than that. How many machines are there usually, in a busy bank?

DONNIE:     2 or 3, sometimes 5.

DICK:       Right. And behind them there's a little room, so they're all connected.

DONNIE:     Ya, but

DICK:       And how many banks are there in the city?

BILLY:      A lot.

DONNIE:     I don't / understand how

DICK:       And if my little plan works—and it will, believe me—we could do a couple of banks a day. And if we fly to another city, we do it again. And again. And again.

            *(Silence.)*

BUG:        Fuck...

DONNIE:     Jesus.

BILLY:      How do we empty the machines?

DICK:       Thank you. These fucks had already spent their cut.

DONNIE:     No I was wonderin'

DICK:       Donnie, we start with you. You do your regular thing somewhere, and get us some cards. We pick a bank, a busy one—one where we can park right nearby, Bug you'll have to get us a car *(BUG nods.)*—and the four of us go together. We sit in the car, and watch the bank, and wait.

    *(Beat.)*

Donnie goes in, makes a withdrawal for 60 bucks— so we have the receipt. Then he makes a couple more withdrawals, 'n a couple more, from different accounts, for a total of 600 bucks. Six hundred dollars. Comes back to the car. Gives the money to Billy.

DONNIE:    What?

DICK:    Listen. Billy takes the money, goes back in, goes up to the customer service counter there, and does a number on one of the bank women. Gives her this sort of shocked but very honest story about how he can't believe it, but he just tried to withdraw sixty bucks from one of the machines, and oh my god—it gave me six hundred by mistake. Look. And he shows her the money, the 600—and the receipt we have that says 60 bucks. Remember? And says, "At first I was gonna just take it, but then I thought no, I can't do that"…and then you give her the money.

DONNIE/BUG:   No way! / Wait a fuckin'

DICK:    Listen! *(Emphatically.)* He gives her the money.
He gives her the money, and he tells her which machine it was, and leaves. And comes back to the car. And we wait.

BILLY:    I give her the six hundred.

DICK:    Yes. You give her the money. And we wait…
We wait.

    *(Beat.)*

BILLY:    For…

DICK:    For the repairmen! The men come—bank employees—come to fix this fucking machine that is giving out hundreds of dollars—bank dollars— that thank God that guy came in and told us about—these men come—these guys are not guards, they are not Brinks guys, they are not armed—am I making myself clear? They have no guns. They enter the bank, followed closely by Bug and myself, whom no one has seen yet—both of whom do have guns—we have guns somewhere don't we Bug? *(BUG nods.)*—yes we have big guns, and we follow our friendly bank repairmen back behind the machines, and with our guns we persuade these guys to empty all the money into our handy duffel bags; we gag our friends, we tie them up—do NOT kill them Bug—we leave them back there where everyone thinks they are repairing away, and we calmly walk out of the bank and into the running car. And on our merry way. Home to count, or on to another bank. "'Nother one before lunch boys? Sure, why not!"

*(Beat.)*

Any questions?

*(Beat.)*

BILLY:     They have no guns.

DICK:      None. Believe me. I hung around those fucking machines for weeks, watching everybody come and go, and no, these repair guys are like plumbers. When they load the things, it's like Fort Knox; but when one breaks down, these two guys waddle in like T.V. repairmen. I'm stakin' out these banks, doing my wino number, and people—unbeliev-able—are throwing money at me! You beg for it—nothin'—but just lie there lookin' around—I made like 40 bucks! No. No guns.

*(Pause.)*

DONNIE:    And he gives her the six hundred?

DICK:      YES DONNIE WILL YOU FUCK OFF ABOUT THAT MONEY! Look honey, that's peanuts. It's nothing. If you go in, and say this machine's not working, they say thanks, and stick a note on it saying out of order. But if you go in and say that machine just gave me 600 of your dollars by

|  | mistake, they thank you and quietly freak out, and the fix-it guys are there in about twenty fucking minutes. Get it? |
|---|---|
| DONNIE: | Ya. |
| DICK: | O.K... Bug, any problems? |
| BUG: | Ya. Why do we need him. *(Gestures towards BILLY.)* |
| DICK: | I marvel at you. If Donnie takes the money up to the bank lady, looking the way he does—no offence now, but you look like you got about two days to live—lookin' like that, they'd call an ambulance. You or I walk in, and it's like the stars of *America's Most Wanted*—it'd be an orgy of 911 dialling. Uh uh. He walks in, they look, they smile, he smiles back, they get a little interested maybe, and he starts. He is our ticket. To no alarms. No fuss. He looks like Joe College. The guy next door that they shoulda fucked. He has an ability with women. |
| BUG: | I can talk to a woman. |
| DICK: | Oh ya, you're a real charmer. |
| BUG: | No one has complained yet. |
| DICK: | Oh no, no complaints. At least not from the ones— oh fuck—*(To DONNIE.)* do you believe this? What about—unless you've blocked it out—what about Darlene Wahby? |
| DONNIE: | *(Groans.)* |
| BUG: | Never mind. |
| DICK: | No, no, I think the story needs to be told, to demonstrate your way, your gift with women. |
| BUG: | She was a pig. |
| DICK: | *(Laughing.)* That didn't stop you. She was a ditch-pig. The only thing keeping her alive was Greenpeace. |
| DONNIE: | Where did their little "exchange" take place? |

*(Both laugh.)*

**BUG:** *(Enjoying it.)* You both fuck off now.

**BILLY:** No tell me what happened.

**DICK:** Well, a couple of years ago we were all partying, at Joan's I think,

**DONNIE:** At Christmas! *(They tease BUG with the story.)*

**DICK:** Yes, on Christmas eve, and he decides in his drunken, heavy-duty drugged delirium that he needs a woman...so he looks around, and picks Darlene instead. So it's really late, or early, anyway everyone has either passed out or fucked off, and they start doin' it right there on the living room floor.

**DONNIE:** An' he's not even awake eh? 'cause he was so out of it, so stoned an' stuff—but his body is still movin'— reflexes or somethin', so he's doin' it—barely—and as he's doin' it, on top of her...he throws up.

**DICK:** Ooooohhh.

**DONNIE:** So gross! So then of course, he rolls off her, and passes out.

**DICK:** Cold. Needless to say, she was not pleased. Barf in her hair, she plots her revenge.

**DONNIE:** Revenge!

**DICK:** *(Laughing.)* We come down the next morning, to find Bug, on his back,

**DONNIE:** right where she left him

**DICK:** On the rug, with a great big Wahby shit right there! *(Indicates his chest.)*

**DONNIE:** She shit on him!

**BILLY:** No.

**DICK/DONNIE:** YES!

DICK: A little thank you for his night of magic.

BUG: Fuck you.

DICK: Merry Christmas!

> *(All laugh.)*

> *(As it subsides…)*

BUG: *(To BILLY.)* You think that's funny?

BILLY: *(Laughing.)* What?

BUG: What are you laughin' at.

BILLY: What.

BUG: I'm just wonderin'—if you were laughin' at me.

BILLY: No Bug. I wasn't. *(Very serious.)*

BUG: You weren't.

BILLY: No. I wasn't laughing at you.

BUG: That's good.

BILLY: I wasn't laughing at the story.

BUG: Good.

BILLY: I was just laughin'—wonderin'…when the last time was you got shit-faced.

> *(Beat. All laugh except BUG. BUG dives at BILLY, but before he can get to him, BILLY is up and behind his chair, with his knife, something flashy, drawn. All freeze.)*

DICK: Now boys. Let's all just relax a bit here. We were just havin' a little fun Bugboy.

> *(Pause.)*

Why don't we all sit down and have another beer. Talk some more about our little caper…our money. We need each other. Bug! We need him alive for a little while longer. You hear me?

BILLY:      I got the fuckin' knife!

DICK:       I see that—but he doesn't care—I've seen him go
            after people with shotguns.

BUG:        I don't like you. I've killed people...

BILLY:      I'll keep that in mind.

            *(Beat.)*

DONNIE:     Hey. *(Makes fixing gesture to DICK.)*

DICK:       Yes. Thank you. Lovely idea. I have something here
            that will interest all of us I'm sure. *(Moves slowly to
            cupboard, removes syringe.)* "Who wants gum?"

DONNIE:     I do.

DICK:       I do.

            *(Beat.)*

            Bug. Donald has found a motherlode of greys in his
            travels. *(Shakes pill bottle.)*

            *(BUG turns at the sound, the room relaxes.)*

DICK:       Good.

BILLY:      I have my own. *(Slowly puts away his knife.)*

DICK:       Wouldn't you love about a gram of this shi—a gram
            of this coursing through those throbbing veins?
            Sure you would.

BILLY:      *(Moving to jacket.)* Mine is all ready. *(Removes
            prepared syringe.)*

DICK:       Always be prepared.

BILLY:      Be my guest.

DICK:       After you.

            *(BILLY sits, and places his right hand between his
            crossed legs, injecting between his thumb and index
            finger. He offers BUG the syringe.)*

DONNIE:      Dick?

DICK:        *(To BILLY.)* Allow me. *(Taking syringe.)* What. *(To DONNIE. BUG bares leg.)*

             *(Beat.)*

DONNIE:      Nothin'.

             *(DICK fixes BUG's leg, then his own foot. Gives DONNIE the syringe. DONNIE squirts a bit into the air, then does his own forearm. BUG paces a bit, then lies down. They all settle.)*

             *(Beat.)*

DICK:        That's better...thanks Billy, very nice. Now let's all share some quiet time...with that money. *(Slowly.)* Bug here, says he's going to go and...and buy himself a farm...or a ranch I guess—is more appropriate.

             *(The sound of a herd of running horses starts under very quietly, builds slowly.)*

             A horse ranch...in the mountains. Bugboy is going to be a horse breeder. He fancies himself a champion horse man. *(Sound is now quite audible.)* Breakin' them...trainin' them...racin'...sellin' ...mustangs...colts...mares... *(Sound of the herd rises to a roar, no one moves, after about seven seconds at this maximum volume, it begins to fade gradually to silence.)*

             *(Pause.)*

             *(BILLY looks around, gets up, moves around room. BUG scratches scalp, DONNIE lights a cigarette.)*

DONNIE:      What was in that?

DICK:        That was one heavy duty kick.

             *(Beat.)*

BILLY:       Just a little high-octane I like to mix up, when I know I'm gonna be with friends.

DICK:         Fuck...I think I saw your life pass before my eyes.

BILLY:        Why mess around when you can do the real thing?

DONNIE:       I'm not supposed to...

              *(Beat.)*

BILLY:        Don't you guys worry about sharing?

DICK:         What?

BILLY:        Needles... You know—gettin' AIDS an' stuff.

DONNIE:       Oh no, we all know that we're—that we don't—
              from being inside, everybody's so paranoid eh? so
              most people got, or get tested—so we know that we
              don't...we know.

DICK:         Yes, thank our lucky stars again for that
              government hospitality. That, and the fact that
              since we've been released, none of us has actually
              had sex for a long, long time. With anybody.

BUG:          Speak for yourself.

DICK:         And just to make sure, whenever we do share, we
              always make Donnie go last, 'cause nobody knows
              what he's got.

DONNIE:       I'm the one that spends all the time in hospitals,
              remember? I know.

BILLY:        Is there a lot of that inside?

DONNIE:       *(Looking at BUG, whose eyes remain closed.)* Um...a lot
              of what?

BILLY:        You know...

DICK:         *(Treading carefully. To BILLY.)* It's not something we
              talk about. Whatever happens inside, is private. It
              almost never happens outside. And with this
              group—nothing happens—period. The last
              woman to touch one of us, died at Woodstock.

              *(Beat.)*

BUG:          What did you say?

BILLY:      What.

BUG:        What did you say?

BILLY:      I was just wonderin' / if when you were

BUG:        *(Sits up.)* What the fuck am I hearin' here. What the FUCK is goin' on here?

DICK:       Bug.

BUG:        Are you tellin' me that you've never done time before?

BILLY:      Uh...ya.

            *(The following three lines are all spoken together.)*

BUG:        WHAT THE FUCK IS GOIN' ON HERE?

DICK:       JUST FUCKIN' SETTLE DOWN—

DONNIE:     YA I THOUGHT IT WAS PRETTY WEIRD TOO—

BUG:        *(Standing.)* I CAN'T FUCKIN' BELIEVE THAT YOU WOULD EVEN THINK OF talkin' about anything, let alone a job—with some asshole / who has never even

DICK:       Just shut up. SHUT UP SHUT UP AND LISTEN TO ME.

BUG:        Listen to what? Listen to you, you asshole? You fuckin' dare bring me in here not a week after I'm out—involved with some fuckin' greenhorn slime *(Indicating BILLY.)* and this *(Indicating DONNIE.)* fuckin' pathetic excuse for a

DICK:       Are you finished? 'Cause if you are, I'll tell you that he is perfect for this job. We need someone who looks like that, AND he has told us about lots of jobs that he has pulled in other places, and surprise surprise he hasn't been caught yet—so that makes him stupid? That makes him a liability? Or not worthy of our company? Fuck Bug, you're the one we should be worried about here. Every time you set foot out the door you end up doin' time. Well maybe this one is different eh? Maybe this one is so

different, and so easy, and so beautifully Simple—
that even YOU won't get caught. And because it's
different, and so big, maybe we need some new
people on this one. And I'm including you in this
because you are my friend, and because I need you
to go in there with me and take the place—I need
your experience.

*(Beat.)*

BUG: You need your fuckin' head examined, is what you
need. He doesn't know code. He would break code.

DICK: He won't break—

BILLY: What's code?

BUG: *(Groans.)* Oh.

DICK: Code is not squealing on each other. Guys that have
done time—it's like a brotherhood—a guy that has
been inside will NEVER inform, or accuse, or tell on
another guy…ever. That's code.

BILLY: Fine. I won't break code.

BUG: You won't have the chance.

DICK: He doesn't believe you because you haven't done
time. People that haven't been inside will say
anything to stay out. If you've already served…

BILLY: I won't break code. I won't have to. 'Cause we
won't get caught.

*(Beat.)*

DONNIE: I believe him.

BUG: Oh fuck. You believe in fucking Santa Claus.

BILLY: Ya and you believe in Fairies, don't you.

DICK: *(Grabs BUG.)* NO. Bug.
*(To BILLY.)* Do you WANT to die?

BUG: Oh he's gonna die all right.

BILLY: We'll see who goes first.

| | |
|---|---|
| BUG: | You fuckin' goof.<br>I'm gettin' the fuck outa here. |
| DICK: | Bug.<br>Bugboy. |

*(BUG exits. DICK follows him.)*

Bug. Fuck. Just hold your fuckin' horses. *(He is gone.)*

*(Pause. DONNIE and BILLY sit in silence. After about five seconds we hear, from outside:)*

| | |
|---|---|
| BUG: | FUCK IT! |
| DICK: | O.K. |

*(Beat. BILLY gets up and closes the door.)*

| | |
|---|---|
| BILLY: | You don't have to be afraid of him. |
| DONNIE: | What? |
| BILLY: | Bug. You don't have to be afraid that he's gonna hurt you. |
| DONNIE: | You don't know him. |
| BILLY: | I know his type. They don't scare me. |

*(Beat. He moves closer.)*

I'm just telling you that now that I'm around, you don't have to worry about Bug anymore.

| | |
|---|---|
| DONNIE: | And why is that. |
| BILLY: | 'Cause I'll take care of him. |

*(Beat.)*

And I'll take care of you.

| | |
|---|---|
| DONNIE: | I can take care of myself, thanks. |
| BILLY: | I can get you anything you want, any morphine, any other drug, any amount. You want more of that stuff we just did? |

DONNIE:    What are you talking about?

BILLY:     I'm just telling you that I'll get you anything you
           need. Whatever you want.

               *(Beat.)*

DONNIE:    Why?

BILLY:     Why what?

DONNIE:    Why would you do that.

               *(Pause. BILLY smiles.)*

BILLY:     Why do you think?

DONNIE:    *(Rising, moving towards door.)* I don't, I don't, I don't
           have a fuckin' clue what you're talking to me about,
           but I know that I gotta get goin' an'—

BILLY:     *(Following him.)* So where you gonna go?

DONNIE:    What?

BILLY:     Where you going?

DONNIE:    You said—

BILLY:     I said I'd take care of you. You're smarter than these
           guys, and you don't deserve that shit Bug gives
           you. So I'm just telling you that I'll protect you from
           him. I'll take care of him…

               *(Beat.)*

           You don't need these guys Donnie.
           Fuck 'em. They're just using you.

               *(Beat.*

           You and me, we'd be quite a pair. You get the
           money, I get the stuff. We'd be laughing. Let's get
           out of here. Just you and me…

               *(Beat. They are near the door.)*

           It doesn't have to be bad.

DONNIE:    You don't know anything about it.

*(DICK bursts through the door, moving to the kitchen to get another beer.)*

DICK:      He's in. He'll be all right. He's in. He knows this is the best thing he's ever heard. By far.

DONNIE:    Dick. I uh…I gotta go.

DICK:      You runnin' out too?

DONNIE:    No, no man, No I think it's good—I think it's—fuck I'm in all the way. I like it.

DICK:      You do?

DONNIE:    *(Moving towards him.)* Oh ya! I wanna I wanna try it. I wanna do it, an' get like hundreds of fuckin' thousands of dollars and buy new everything! Kidneys, lungs, the whole fuckin' outfit.

DICK:      Good. I wanna start on Friday—I'll get Bug to get the car, and we'll see you Friday morning, banks'll be real busy.

DONNIE:    O.K. good. Good…Friday, sounds good. I'm ready. But I have an N.A. meeting at eight—fuck I gotta go.

           *(He exits.)*

BILLY:     *(Calling after him.)* I'll give you a ride.

           *(Going for his jacket.)*

DICK:      So…will we see you Friday?

BILLY:     Oh…ya, sure, I'll be there, ya, I think it'll work.

DICK:      That's good. You all right?

BILLY:     Oh ya. I'm O.K.

DICK:      Good.
           Listen…uh…take it easy with Bug.

BILLY:     I don't have a problem with Bug.
           I think he has a problem with me.

DICK:      Well I don't want any problems.

*(Beat.)*

BILLY:          O.K. No problem.

DICK:           Good… No problems at all.

> *(BILLY exits. DICK goes to stereo, searches for a tape. He finds it, puts it in, presses play. It is "Born to Run". He dances to it gently, singing along, laughing as he finds DONNIE's bottle of Roxanol. Lights fade to black, music continues.)*

# Scene Five

*(The car outside the bank. It is an old boat of a car, the top removed for sightlines. DICK is at the wheel, BUG is in the front passenger seat, and BILLY is in the back seat, directly behind BUG. They are waiting for DONNIE in silence. After about ten seconds, BUG groans and slides down in his seat. BILLY is looking stage left. After another pause, DONNIE hurries on from stage left, and gets in behind DICK.)*

DICK: *(Not turning around.)* D'you get it?

DONNIE: Well ya, but I had I had a fuck of a time in there.

*(The following three lines are spoken together.)*

BILLY: Whatta ya mean?

BUG: I knew somethin' would fuck up.

DICK: What happened.

DONNIE: No, nothin' fucked up, it just—it was just a nightmare in there with so many people an' everythin', an' me tryin' to use all these different cards and stuff eh? an' get the money with all these fuckin' people breathin' down your neck, and wonderin' why you're takin' so long. An' oh I shoulda wrote it down—how much I was gonna take from each one to make up 600 bucks

DICK: D'you get it?

DONNIE: Oh ya, ya I got it, it just was hard 'cause I had to keep countin' it to see how much I had, an' then I kept losin' track an' gettin' the cards all mixed up, and all these fuckin' uptight assholes are lookin' at me, and doin' all this heavy sighin', because I'm using up their lunch-hour, makin' them stand in line there an' wait' an' wait for the other machines, an' there's always some old guy at the machine who's never done it before eh? an' he's reading every line of the instructions really slow an' making everybody crazy an'

BUG:        Just give us the money.

DICK:       Give the 600 bucks / to Billy.

DONNIE:     O.K., O.K. I got it, I will, I will—thank God those people had money in their accounts, I was thinkin' that when I was in there eh, what if the cards that I got, the people had no money, *(Laughing.)* had nothin' in their accounts, an' I'd be pushin' withdraw, withdraw like a freak eh? an' the machine goes No, No, an' I goes

DICK:       Just count out the money for Billy, and give him the receipt that says 60 bucks.

DONNIE:     Oh ya, I got that, I got those too, I got a whole whack of 'em here, *(Pulls receipts and bank cards and money from jacket pocket.)* and…this…one is the one for 60 bucks for you, *(Gives it to BILLY.)* and this is the money. You think we should recount it to make sure there's 600? 'cause I think I ended up with a little more

BUG:        More!

BILLY:      Give me the money

DICK:       Yes fuck, count out the money and hurry up, yer yakking up a storm like you're—are you speeding you asshole? I told you—no shit until after the job.

DONNIE:     No no I'm just excited this is just so exciting like in a movie or somethin' an' I'm shakin'—

            *(BUG turns and looks at him.)*

            O.K. O.K. I'm countin' it out, I'm doin' it, O.K. *(On seat between himself and BILLY, he lays down the money.)* Two four six eight one hundred, two four six eight…two…four…

BILLY:          No that's two hundred two four six eight

DONNIE:         *(Counts with him.)* four six eight three, two four six eight, four, and two four six eight five and two four six eight SIX! There! You take that, an' I still got two four six eight eighty bucks left over Dick, that I got 'cause I got a bit mixed up

DICK:           You can keep that / for your trouble—

BUG:            No split it. He should split it four ways.

DICK:           What? / What are you talking about he should split

DONNIE:         Oh ya, ya I was gonna split it—I would never keep it for myself, that's why I told you all that I got some extra so you wouldn't think... *(BILLY is recounting the money.)* you wouldn't think that I was tryin' to rip ya's off or anythin', 'cause we're all in this together I think so everybody gets a cut—so there's one for you *(Hands bill to BUG.)* and one for you *(Hands bill to DICK.)* and one for you *(Hands bill to BILLY.)* an' don't get it mixed up with the other stuff, and one for me. Oh ya that's only fair.

DICK:           *(To BUG.)* Asshole. This is shit. This is fuckin' diddly. Quit thinking small time, this isn't smoke money we're talking here, this isn't nickel and dimin'

BUG:            I just wanna make sure I get somethin' / out of this stupid

DICK:           Oh you'll get something, you'll get something you fuckin' pinhead, you'll get ten to twelve if you / don't stop tryin' to fuck it up with your

BUG:            Don't fuckin' talk to me about gettin' anything but my fuckin' share, and that's part of my share. My money.

DICK:           O.K. O.K. you... Just take the twenty measly bucks and go buy yourself something real nice.

BILLY:          Maybe he can get a little pony for his farm.

                *(BUG snaps around in the seat to attack BILLY.)*

DICK:      BUG! Bug. Don't you fuckin' hit him just before he has to go in that bank, and get and give that money, and talk to one of the— Don't you fuckin' dare fuck this up! Sit down.
Come on. Just sit down and watch with me.

*(BUG turns around, slumps in seat)*

Thank you. Jesus Christ you can't fuck with him before he goes in there. I already explained the whole thing to you in very simple words: he's the one who goes into the fuckin' bank.

*(Pause.)*

BUG:      I think we should split the 600.

*(The next four speeches are spoken at the same time.)*

DONNIE:      Ya I was thinkin' maybe we should just split it up too 'cause it seems real busy in there and I'm not sure about this plan o' yours, don't you call me an asshole you asshole I'm the one who got the I can SO count I just was nervous sitting in this shitbox with that fuckin' animal

DICK:      Split it? Split the fucking 600 bucks? Jesus Fucking Christ I've never heard such The plan is fine. An' if you weren't so stupid yes fuckin' stupid maybe we would've had this kind of just get in that fucking bank

BILLY:      No way are we splitting this shitty little bit of cash just because some fucking ugly goof—I can't believe this—the plan is not fine as long as this asshole who can't even fuckin' count, and this cocksucker who shoulda been dead a long time ago are part of this

BUG:      I don't think this fuckin' asshole Yes split the 600 bucks because this whole idea is so fuckin' fucked— and No Way can you give a cent to this Stupid? you calling me Stupid with this shit in the back seat I'll kill you I'm gonna kill you *(To BILLY.)*

DICK:      *(Grabs DONNIE and BUG and shakes them while*

*screaming.)* SHUT UP! Shut up. Everybody just shut the fuck up.

*(Pause, then quietly.)*

Now I don't care what you three assholes think of this plan, well yes I do, but if you don't think it's gonna work, you can just get the fuck out of this car, and walk away right now. We have the money, and the guns, and I'll finish the fucker myself, if any or all of you pathetic freaks of nature want to get out, just get out now, and go back to your sad sorry lives, and pretend that you never heard of any of this. Anyone wants out, get out now.

*(Pause.)*

But if you stay, I don't want to hear a word

BUG:        Just

DICK:       Not a fucking SOUND about this not working, or this guy doesn't like me, or who's the stupidest, or who stole what—I can't believe what I brought together here. We are sitting on the biggest gold mine that anybody's ever dreamed of, this thing is so simple, so purely right—and you three stooges are gonna fuck it up 'cause you don't have any faith, Faith—that something could come along, be dropped in your lap, that could change your life forever. You gotta get over your petty little differences, and your fears, and you just gotta believe in this, just for now, just for a half an hour please, you gotta believe that there is a way out of this, an easy way for all of us *all of us* to get what we want. Now.

*(Beat.)*

Is anybody out?

*(Pause.)*

O.K. Good. Good.
Billy, I want you to take the money, and the receipt, as planned, take it into the bank, and up to the

Customer Service counter. Tell the woman who comes up to help you, exactly what has happened, as we discussed. And give her the money. Just give her the money. I know that may be the hardest part of the whole thing so far, but you have to believe, to understand that that is the key. Give her the money. Then you come back here. You got it?

BILLY: Ya.

DICK: Give her the money. Come back here. And then we wait. Simple.

DONNIE: Dick?

DICK: What.

DONNIE: I'm...I...I don't feel very good.

DICK: What do you mean? How bad are you?

DONNIE: I dunno. I just started to get kinda dizzy, an' I'm sweatin'

DICK: Don't give me a—what do you think is wrong?

DONNIE: I dunno...but while he's in there, can I, do you think I could maybe maybe go an'...take these wallets back?

BUG: (Groans.)

DICK: No. No Donnie 'cause something might happen to you, and we can't risk it. You might get sick, or hit by a car, or you might even get caught, you don't know maybe one of those ladies has noticed her wallet is missing, and the cops might be there, and we just can't risk you getting out of the car right this second. O.K?

DONNIE: Oh that's O.K. Ya I get it, ya I can see that but...ya know I'd feel a lot better, if maybe I could get these people back their I.D. an' stuff

BILLY/BUG/
DICK: (Together.) Jesus.

DICK: Uh no, Donnie, I know ya feel bad, but right now is

not the best time. Tell ya what—after we have the money, we'll pull by the church and see if any of them are still there, and if they're gone, you can take that stuff right to their houses, you have their addresses probably in their wallets, you can take it right to them, and maybe even slip in a hundred bucks for them, to make it up to them, for their trouble.

DONNIE:     Uh I don't think I'd go that far. But I might bring 'em back to them, that sounds good. Ya I like that.

DICK:       Good boy. Good. Right. Now.
            *(To BILLY.)* You ready?

BILLY:      Yup.

DICK:       O.K. man...go give 'er.

DONNIE:     Good luck eh.

            *(BUG leans forward, head in hands.)*

BILLY:      *(Gets out of car, leans back in.)* See ya in Mexico.

            *(Laughs, slams door. He puts the earphones of his walkman on his head, pushes "Play". Intense modern rock music in. He crosses into the bank area, looks around, the lights fade on the car.)*

# Scene Six

*(BILLY enters a pool of light, representing the bank counter. He removes the headphones, pushes "Stop" on the walkman, the music stops. Pause.)*

BILLY:

Excuse me? Miss? I was just wondering if you could help me... Thanks. You're not gonna believe this, it's so amazing—probably the weirdest thing that's ever happened to me—well no, not the weirdest— but definitely the weirdest in a bank. Have you worked here long? 'Cause I wanted to make sure I was talking to someone important—'cause what happened to me is pretty major. Oh good. Good. *(He smiles.)*
Well see, I just went up to one of your machines out there eh, the one at this end? Ya. They're great those things aren't they?—they sure speed up the whole process—I hardly ever come inside any more. Oh my name is Tom by the way, Tom Richards...and you are... *(Reading name-tag.)* ...Ms. Amore... Amoré—what is that Italian? It's nice.
Anyway—I go up to the machine, just now, and I put in my card, and I go to withdraw some money from my account—for some groceries—and I punch in 60 dollars—and this is the amazing part— the machine—believe it—didn't give me 60— *(Laughs, looks around, whispers.)* It gave me six hundred. Ya, 600—I know, I can't believe it either,I wouldn't've believed it if I didn't have it—ya look. *(Takes money and receipt from pocket.)* See? Yes...it is a lot of money.

*(Beat.)*

The receipt? Ya, right here. For 60. I guess it just added a zero or something—I know *(Laughs.)* think if I'd tried to get a hundred—or more! Ya...well I thought of it. Well actually—this happened about 10 minutes ago. I walked around a bit. I was kind of in shock—it was like being at one of those machines—ya know—those betting machines? with the handle? Slot Machines! Right—like standing at a slot machine and Bing Bing Bing—3 cherries—and I hit the jackpot—ya! and the twenties come flying out—like I'm in Las Vegas— ever been to Vegas? No? Oh it's great—ya, I know, I thought so too, but it's not—it's crazy—a really way-out-there kind of place, but fun, ya know? Ya... Well as I said I thought of just walking, walking away with it all... God it's hot in here eh? 'Cause I'll tell ya...I could really use that money right now. Well I'm not working, ya I just got laid off. Me? Oh, I'm a teacher—ya—high school, and I guess there's a lot of phys. ed. teachers right now— I just came in one day, and they told me they didn't need me any more—just like that. But you must be pretty secure here eh? Your job? No? But banks are always making money. *(Laughing.)* Well not if they keep giving it away like this! Anyway I really need the money, but I thought about it, and I thought No—no I couldn't do that—'cause what if the people that work here, have to make up the difference at the end of the day—and I wouldn't want to do that to you. No. And I'm Catholic too. Oh, are you? *(Smiles.)* Well then you know what I mean. And well, my mom's not well right now, and I'm trying to take care of her and that eh? and— she's got bad kidneys—ya real bad...and she's waiting for a transplant, but they haven't been able to find a match yet—so I...I— *(He stops.)*

Shit.

*(Beat. He does not cry.)*

Sorry.

*(Beat.)*

No, I'm all right. I just...it just...ever have the feeling that the bottom just dropped out? Of everything? I get it once in a while—more often lately—where I'm just going along, everything's going fine, everything's cool, and then—*(Dropping gesture.)*—it just goes—like the pit of my stomach just—drops away—gone—and I kind of lose it— lose everything... That's what just happened. Bottom dropped out. *(Beat.)* My life.

*(Beat.)*

Ya see I'm kind of sick myself. Well that's the weird part, 'cause I'm not really—yet—so I feel sort of marked or something—like I've got a secret—but hell, everybody has a secret or two eh? But mine's bad...

*(Beat.)*

Amoré—there's a song about that isn't there? Ya... What's your first name? Alma. That's beautiful. D'you know what that means in Spanish? Hope. *(Mouths the name Alma.)* That's lovely... Jeez I'm sorry for taking up so much of your time here, going on about all my stuff. You seem like a really good person Alma—I come in to tell you about my little adventure with the machine, and you get the whole shootin'... I'd like to ask you—I was wondering if you'd like to go out with me sometime...

*(Beat.)*

Oh. Well, no. I didn't think you would.

*(Backs away a bit.)*

Well... I guess I should be going now. It's hot in here with this jacket on. Thanks for helping me... No I'm O.K....

DICK:  *(Taped voice-over.)* And you give her the money.

BILLY:  Ya. I'm sure. *(Backs away another step, looks around.)*

DICK:  *(V.O.)* Give her the money.

BILLY:  I'll call you sometime...here.

*(Beat.)*

DICK:          *(V.O.)* Give her the money.

               *(Pause.)*

BILLY:         I guess I should give you this.

               *(Holds out money to her, walking towards counter
               as lights fade to black.)*

# Scene Seven

*(DICK, BUG and DONNIE are waiting in the car, in silence.)*

DICK: How you feeling now Donnie? You all right?

DONNIE: Ya.

DICK: You sure?

DONNIE: Oh ya, I'm...I'll be O.K.

DICK: What do you mean you'll *be* O.K.—are you not O.K. now? How come you're sweatin'? And you're all pale and sort of splotchy. Are you having some kind of crisis or something? Do you need some pills?

BUG: He needs a good shot.

DICK: Are you fucked up? Are you Jonesin' already?

DONNIE: Oh no, no, I'm fine, no not that, Jeez—I don't hardly ever do that anymore, no I'm just sort of hot eh? I'm findin' it hard to breathe in the car can I open the window? just a bit? *(DICK nods.)* No, no I'm doin' O.K., I just sometimes have trouble with my one kidney—like it sort of breaks down sometimes, and doesn't work as well an' then I get all toxic eh? an' that can sort of make me feel like I'm failin' or somethin'—but no I'm all right—well actually the main thing right now—the main trouble is that I really gotta take a piss bad.

DICK/BUG: *(Together.)* Oh!

*(Pause.)*

DONNIE: *(Looking off left.)* What's takin' him so long?

DICK: I'm sure he's doing just fine in there.

DONNIE: Fuck here he comes!

> *(They all jump, and look left. BILLY comes in from Stage Left, gets in behind BUG.)*

DONNIE: Well?

BILLY: What.

DONNIE: D'you get it?

BILLY: Get what?

DONNIE: I mean give it to her?

DICK: Shut up. *(To BILLY.)* How'd it go?

BILLY: Just fine. Just like you said. Like you wanted. *(He looks off left.)* I gave her the money—gave her this big story about how amazed I was first, then we talked a bit...and I gave her the money. She was real nice. It went just fine.

DICK: Good. That's a boy.

BILLY: Actually I think she and I are—gonna be going out together.

DONNIE/BUG: What! / You fucker!

DICK: That's O.K. That's good. That's exactly what he was supposed to do. She ain't gonna push any alarm bells if she's gonna maybe be dating the guy who just came in / with the money

BUG: He can't fuckin' go back in there—3 days after we hit the place for maybe a hundred grand, he can't walk back in there and say hey remember me, I gave you the 600 bucks, let's go—

BILLY: I'm not going back in there asshole—you and Dick are going back in for the hit—she won't connect me with you guys.

DICK: I dunno…he may be right

BUG: Of course I'm right

DICK: Maybe you don't want to be going back anywhere near the place for a while.

BILLY: I gave her my phone number.

(Beat. All freeze.)

I'm kidding! (DICK and BUG groan. BILLY laughs.) Actually I used this sick routine I do. It always does the trick.

DICK: It doesn't matter what you told her—she may put together that you going in with the money was what brought those repairmen to the bank—

DONNIE: Are you sick? (BILLY shakes his head "No.")

DICK: —and we don't want to take any chances of you getting picked up when you call this woman,

BILLY: Alma.

DONNIE: Alma! He even knows her name!

DICK: Can't take any chances with Alma, sorry.

BUG: Did you tell her your name too, Fuck?

BILLY: No, I didn't… Faggot.

BUG: (Turning on him.) I told you once asshole. Don't push it. 'Cause if we go, we're gonna go.

BILLY: I'm ready. Let's go.

BUG: (Spoken at the same time as DICK's first two words following.) Don't fuck

DICK: DON'T FUCKIN' START FIGHTIN' IN THE CAR. Jesus. Turn around. Can you two leave each other's throats for ten minutes? Twenty minutes? Please? This is the part where we wait remember? Everything has worked fucking perfectly so far—and I can't have you two fucking it up BEFORE we get the money. Jesus. Now everybody just sit down, and shut up, and wait. Look around for a bank car, or truck, and some guys with tool boxes. That's what we're here for. Not to get lucky, or get killed. Billy, I'm sorry, but I'd rather you didn't call on that woman for that date.

BILLY:        I'm not gonna.

DICK:        Thank you, I didn't think you would—but that's good. Now that we have that settled, we'll all just sit, and wait. Keep a look out for those guys. We got the guns here *(Gestures to bag at BUG's feet.)*, and we're gonna go in, and get it—as soon as those guys show. So shut up—and watch.

            *(Pause for 15 seconds.)*

DONNIE:    How did you get her to go on a date with you?

BUG:         AH! *(Goes for one of the guns at his feet.)*

DICK:        Fuck. *(He wrestles the gun out of BUG's hands.)* Donnie. Shut up! If you ever mention that again I'll kill you. I'll kill you myself—you understand? Now just shut the fuck. Don't say anything. Jesus Christ Almighty.

            *(Pause. They wait. BUG takes out smokes and a lighter from his pocket, lights one. They wait. DONNIE coughs. Beat. DONNIE coughs again. BUG opens his window a bit. Blows the smoke out. DONNIE has a coughing fit.)*

BILLY:        Jesus—you can't fucking smoke in the car. He's dyin' back here, but he's too afraid to say anything 'cause he'll get killed if he does.

DICK:        Bug, don't smoke in the car.

BUG:         He smokes.

DICK:        I know he smokes, but today he's not feeling well, and we can't have him coughing up a lung, and attracting the attention of the people walking by—so don't smoke.

            *(Beat, BUG smokes.)*

BUG:            I could kill him. *(As a suggestion.)*

                *(DONNIE coughs again.)*

DICK:           No, because you're gonna get blood all over us, *(Laughing.)* and the car, and we can't be sittin' here in the Buick, waitin', with a dead guy in the back.

                *(BUG laughs. He takes another drag, butts it out in the ashtray, then flicks the cigarette out his window.)*

                Thank you.

DONNIE:         Thank you.

                *(Beat. DONNIE coughs again. Pause. They watch.)*

                Who's that! *(Pointing down centre. They all look.)*

DICK:           Where?

DONNIE:         Right there—with the bag.

DICK:           That's a fucking mailman, arse.

DONNIE:         Well…

BUG:            Jesus.

                *(Beat.)*

BILLY:          What do they look like, these guys.

DONNIE:         Ya, what do they wear?

DICK:           Well they're not in uniform. The guys I've seen come in—were in bad suits, old suits that they'd rather not be wearing—carrying black or brown leather, big square briefcases—bigger than normal. Probably not in a bank car—maybe in a van.

                *(They watch.)*

DONNIE:         Everybody's in a suit.

DICK:           You'll know them when they come. How long has it been? It hasn't been long enough yet—they can't come right away—just keep looking.

*(Pause.)*

DONNIE:    Hey that guy looks like—isn't that Bingo Waters?

BUG:       Where?

DONNIE:    It is. Beep the horn. HEY!

DICK:      Will you SHUT UP! You can't be screaming at some old freak who just happens to be going by, when you're out on a job. Jesus. Do you think we're just out for a drive here? Are we parked, so you can wave at your friends? Fuck Donnie. You're losing it.

           *(Beat.)*

           And that couldn't have been Bingo anyway. 'Cause for one thing, he's dead, and for another, he never looked that good.

           *(Beat.)*

DONNIE:    Well I think it was him.

           *(Pause.)*

           Dick?

DICK:      What.

DONNIE:    I really gotta go.

DICK:      I'm sorry Buddy, but you can't go right now.

DONNIE:    I just think that I better, 'cause I sometimes I can't hold it as long as—since my one kidney—please

BILLY:     Let him go find a men's room in one of these buildings

DICK:      He can't go wandering around in there and get lost

DONNIE:    I won't get lost

BILLY:     Then let him just get out and piss behind a tree or down a laneway or

DICK:      Oh ya, and then he gets arrested for pissin' outside,

and just happens to have all these extra wallets on
him

DONNIE:     I won't get arrested

BUG:        YOU'RE NOT PISSIN'!

BILLY:      What the fuck's it got to do with you?

BUG:        If I can't smoke, he can't piss.

            *(Beat.)*

DONNIE:     He's just mad 'cause you got that date with that
            woman in the bank.

            *(BUG turns and looks at DONNIE. Then turns
            back.)*

BILLY:      Touché.

DONNIE:     What?

BILLY:      Touché.

DONNIE:     What's that mean?

BILLY:      It's French for touchy.
            Well Bug, pretty soon those guys from the service
            department are gonna come along and, maybe
            while you're in there tying them up, you can try
            and set up a date with one of them. Or hell, while
            you're holding a gun to their heads, you might get
            lucky right there.

            *(Beat. BUG turns and looks at DICK. DONNIE
            moans.)*

DICK:       What's wrong.

DONNIE:     A cop.

DICK:       Where?

DONNIE:     Right there.

BUG:        Ten o'clock.

DICK:       I see him…I see him.

*(Beat.)*

DONNIE:     What do we do?

DICK:       Nothin'. He doesn't see us.

DONNIE:     Oh no.

BUG:        I can't be here man…I can't be with you guys.

DICK:       That copper's gonna just keep on, right on down that side.

BUG:        Dickie, I'm only out a week, my parole, man—fuck.

DICK:       It's O.K. It's O.K., he doesn't see us. There's a lot of cars.

            *(Beat. They watch.)*

DONNIE:     He sees us!

DICK:       He doesn't fuckin' see us. He's just looking.

DONNIE:     I'm gettin' out man—I'm fuckin'

DICK:       Donnie—you're not moving—don't you fuckin' touch that door.

DONNIE:     I got all these cards and wallets on me, / and

DICK:       And if you get out and run he'll be right after you. Just sit tight.

BILLY:      What's the big panic? We're not doing anything.

BUG:        It's a stolen car, asshole.

BILLY:      You stole it.

DONNIE:     He's lookin' right at us.

DICK:       He's not. He's looking at the car. He can't see us from there.

BUG:        And we got a fuckin' bag of shotguns here and we're sittin' outside a bank—

DICK:       The panic, Billy, is 'cause this car is hot, and may

|  |  |
|---|---|
| | have been reported, and the guns, and Bug bein' on parole—if he gets caught with us he's right back in— |
| DONNIE: | He's comin' over here... |
| DICK: | Stay still!—and Donnie's got a few wallets he's borrowed, and...I'm driving without a licence. |
| DONNIE: | You're what? |
| BUG: | You fucker! |
| DICK: | You knew that. I haven't had a licence for years, since that circus job...where we stole the bus? |
| DONNIE: | What's he lookin' at? |
| DICK: | Oh shit! He's looking at the parking sign. Are we illegally parked? |
| BILLY/BUG: | Beautiful. / Fuck. |
| DONNIE: | No, no the sign says *(Looking behind them.)* uh, 7 to 9 a.m. or 3:30 to 6:00 p.m. except on weekends / and holidays... |
| BUG: | What time is it! |
| DONNIE: | No, no, we're O.K....I think. |
| BILLY: | He's not looking at the sign. |
| DICK: | It's O.K. Between nine and three we're O.K. There's other cars here. There's fucking meters. |
| BILLY: | He's looking at that coffee shop. |
| DONNIE: | He is! He's gonna go in. |
| DICK: | He's crossing... Jaywalking I might add...and going into the Donut Delite—Thank you very much. |
| | *(Beat.)* |
| BUG: | Did anybody put anything in the meter? |
| DICK: | Donnie? |

DONNIE: Well there was some time left on it when we pulled in.

DICK: That was half an hour ago.

BUG: Did you not put any of that change in the meter?

DONNIE: No I did, I did…I'm sure I did.

BILLY: There's time on the meter. I can see it. Will you guys fucking relax? It's one cop. If he stops, if he makes us get out—we pop him. And drive off.

DONNIE: Oh no.

DICK: We're not taking out a cop in broad daylight, with two hundred witnesses.

BUG: Anybody gets popped, it's gonna be you.

BILLY: Ya think so eh?

DICK: He won't bother us—he's by himself. Coppers on their own are no problem. They're like bikers, or ethnic types that way; singly they're fine, it's only when they're in groups that there's trouble.

DONNIE: There he is!

DICK: He didn't pay for that.

      *(Beat.)*

BUG: What is he lookin' at?

DICK: He's sees something…

BILLY: Fuck, it's the car!

BUG: What's wrong with the car?

BILLY: What's wrong with it? Jesus, where were you in '72? This fuckin' boat is so old it takes up two parking spots. What is it—the first car you ever drove?

BUG: You fuck off you little

DONNIE: He's coming!

BILLY: *(Laughing.)* And it's.so fuckin' rusted he's probably gonna ask you if it's certified.

DICK: Everybody just sit—don't look at him.

DONNIE: Oh no... *(A whine.)*

BUG: I'm outa here

DICK: No Bug.

BILLY: You fuckin' chicken.

DONNIE: Dick... *(Even more terrified.)*

BUG: I'm goin'. *(He opens his door about two inches.)*

DICK: No! *(He grabs BUG's arm.)*

BILLY: You fuckin' fag chicken shit.

> *(DONNIE takes a huge breath. They freeze for about eight seconds as we hear the cop walk by on their right.)*

DICK: ...and...goodbye...

DONNIE: *(Exhales.)* Oh fuck... Is he gone?

DICK: He's gone. He's all gone.

BILLY: *(Laughing.)* I can't believe it. Buggy was scared shitless.

> *(BUG pushes his door open, and slams it shut. They listen to BILLY laugh.)*

DICK: *(To BUG.)* It's too late, isn't it.

> *(BUG nods.)*

BILLY: Too late for what? For what? It's too late for you Bugboy... You're a dead man.

DICK: *(To BILLY.)* Hey! Do you want to shut the fuck up. I just wish you'd shut that ugly mouth o' yours, before you fuck this whole thing up.

> *(Beat.)*

Do you want to fuck it up? Do you want to have to keep scrambling for shit? Ripping off nurses? Do you wanna live like that? Don't you want this money? I'm talking a shitload of money—don't you want it? Don't you want out of this? That money could mean the end of this life—this running, hustling, fucking killing yourself. Don't you want out?

*(Pause.)*

BILLY:      No.

DICK:       You don't.

BILLY:      No I don't... I want the money...but I don't want out.

*(Beat.)*

DONNIE:    I want out.

*(Pause. DICK turns facing front.)*

BUG:        Donnie...what was that you were telling us while your friend there was in the bank...somethin' he said to you the other night?

*(BILLY looks at DONNIE.)*

DONNIE:    I never said nothin'...

BUG:        Sure ya did...somethin' about you not having to worry about Bug anymore? 'Cause he's gonna take care of me?

DONNIE:    No... I never.

BUG:        What. Were you making it up?

*(Beat.)*

BILLY:      I said it.

BUG:        You did.

BILLY:      Yup.

BUG:        And how were you thinking of taking care of me?

BILLY:    Easy... *(He pops out his blade—reaches into the front seat, slowly passes the knife in front of BUG's face—and leans back again.)*

Come on Bug. Let's do it.
What are you waiting for? Do you want me to start?

*(Beat.)*

COME ON!

*(He pops BUG in the back of the head with his fist. Pause.)*

DICK:    Bug. Bug, just give me five minutes. Give these guys five more minutes to get here. They'll come. It's gotta work Bug. Please. Let it work.

*(Pause. BUG does not move.)*

*(Faster.)* O.K., O.K. now, everybody watch for them 'cause they're comin', I feel them comin'.

DONNIE:    *(Moaning.)* Dick... *(Begins to rock with having to pee.)*

DICK:    Donnie—think about somethin' else... Like... like...movies! What's your favourite one?

DONNIE:    Ah I don't know that's hard...uh...let me think a bit. I like all movies.

DICK:    My favourite is *Cuckoo's Nest*. You know, *One Flew Over the Cuckoo's Nest*? That's a great one. Used to watch that once a month inside. Memorized practically the whole thing.

DONNIE:    Ya I like that one too. I like when they go fishin'

DICK:    Ya that's a classic, always thought that was some of Jack's best work.

DONNIE:    And Billy Bibbet!

DICK:    Yes Donnie, you can be Billy BBBBBibbet—and I'll be Jack, and Bug can be the big Indian

DONNIE:    Chief!

DICK:    and Billy, well...he can be Nurse Ratched. What's your favourite Donnie?

| | |
|---|---|
| DONNIE: | I can't think of it yet…go on to someone else. |
| DICK: | Bug? |

*(Beat.)*

Bug's favourite movie, I know, is *The Misfits*.

| | |
|---|---|
| DONNIE: | *The Misfits*? |
| DICK: | Ya, you know that one—Clark Gable, Monty Clift, all of them lookin' old and like shit, they go up into the mountains |
| DONNIE: | Oh the horses! |
| DICK: | Ya. They try and break wild ponies… Kind of sad that one—but it's got those horses, Bug's ranch in the mountains, and his |
| BUG: | Shut up. |
| DICK: | Bug wants to be Clark Gable, I'll be Monty, Billy— you can be Marilyn Monroe, and Donnie, you can be…Thelma Ritter. |
| DONNIE: | Thelma! |
| DICK: | Ya she's tough. And real smart.<br>What's your favourite Billy? |

*(Beat.)*

Billy passes to you Donnie. Time's up. You gotta tell us now. What is it?

| | |
|---|---|
| DONNIE: | No I can't, there's too many, an'—oh ya—no, that's not the best—O.K. I got one, but I can't tell ya, 'cause you'll laugh. |
| DICK: | We won't laugh. |
| DONNIE: | No way, you'll laugh at me. |
| DICK: | We won't laugh. We all promise that we won't. Bug, Billy, do you guys promise cross your heart hope to die that you won't laugh at Donnie's movie? |

*(Silence.)*

|           | They promise. Tell us what it is. |
|-----------|-----------------------------------|
| DONNIE:   | No I can't. |
| DICK:     | Come on, we all promised. |
| DONNIE:   | I gotta pee! |
| DICK:     | Tell us Donnie. If you tell us, I might let you get out, and |
| DONNIE:   | O.K., O.K. It's—*The Sound of Music.* |

*(Beat. They all laugh except DONNIE, who begins to cry.)*

|           |                                    |
|-----------|------------------------------------|
| BILLY:    | Oh shit, oh No. Don't—stop— |
| DICK:     | It's O.K. Donnie, I'm sorry |
| BILLY:    | Fuck it! He's pissed himself. |

*(DONNIE starts to wail as BUG and BILLY begin to yell simultaneously.)*

|           |                                    |
|-----------|------------------------------------|
| BUG:      | GET OUT! GET HIM OUT! OUT! OUT! |
| BILLY:    | Fuck you. He's not getting out! NO! |

*(DICK grabs one of the sawed-off shotguns from the bag at BUG's feet, points it at BUG and at BILLY, cocks it. All freeze in silence. Beat.)*

|           |                                    |
|-----------|------------------------------------|
| DICK:     | Nobody's getting out until those fuckers come. We'll sit here—and we'll wait. And don't talk. Anybody makes a sound—I'll blow his head off. |

*(Beat. DONNIE cries, one gasp. Beat.)*

|           |                                    |
|-----------|------------------------------------|
| BUG:      | I can't sit here with that smell. |

*(DONNIE ducks.)*

|           |                                    |
|-----------|------------------------------------|
| DICK:     | Would you rather be dead? |
| BUG:      | *(Thinks.)* ...I dunno. |
| BILLY:    | Guys like you prefer the smell of shit, don't they. |

*(DICK re-aims the shotgun at BILLY.)*

BUG: *(Looking in rear-view mirror.)* You are so dead.

DICK: There's gonna be a shit-storm in this car, if you both don't shut the fuck up.

BILLY: *(Ignoring him and lifting knife.)* I'm gonna take your head right off your body…

BUG: Try.

> *(Pause. DICK faces forward, drops gun to his lap. Beat. BILLY grabs BUG from behind, holding his head back with his right arm, his left hand holds the knife at BUG's throat. All freeze.)*

DICK: Maybe we should all just relax a bit, while we figure out what we're gonna do.

> *(Beat.)*

Bug? Don't touch his face. The woman in the bank—will have to identify him when you're done.

BILLY: *(Pointing knife at DICK.)* What are you sayin'?

> *(BUG grabs both of BILLY's wrists, holding them tight. BILLY grunts a little from the effort of resisting, then BUG turns in one movement on to his knees, and pulls BILLY over the front seat, pinning him with his body.)*

DONNIE: NO! *(Grabs at BUG.)*

> *(BUG backhands DONNIE with his right hand, knocking him out against the side window. He takes the knife from BILLY, and stabs him repeatedly in the stomach, while he holds him pinned over the seat. When BILLY stops resisting, BUG throws his body into the back seat. BUG turns facing front and sits. Pause.)*

DICK: Well…that's another fine mess you've gotten us into.

> *(Beat.)*

Now what do we do…

> *(They both look at the bank, off left.)*

Fuckin' banks. They get you comin' and goin'.

*(Beat.)*

Well…give Donnie the knife.

BUG:      What.

DICK:      Put the knife in Donnie's hand. We have to get the fuck out of here, and we aren't bringing them.

*(BUG turns back, takes the knife from BILLY's hand, puts it in DONNIE's. Sits facing front again.)*

Better clean up.

*(He removes two rags from the gun bag, gives one to BUG. DICK wipes the shotgun, and returns it to the bag. BUG cleans any blood off himself. Together, they wipe the front seat area of the car clean of prints.)*

DICK:      The guns.

*(They open their doors with the rags, BUG taking the bag with the guns. They push the doors shut, pocket the rags.)*

DICK:      See ya.

*(They walk away in different directions, leaving BILLY and DONNIE in the back seat. Music in full. Lights fade to black.)*

# Scene Eight

*(It is several months later. Beer and syringes are scattered about DICK's living room. BUG is on the couch, DICK is on the floor. They are laughing.)*

DICK: *(Laughing.)* In your home town.

BUG: Yes asshole. Where was I supposed to go? I didn't have a fuckin' cent.

DICK: Wait—you hit a bank—you tried to hit a bank in your own town—where you grew up.

BUG: Ya, listen—I haven't been back there in 23 years—I walked around for two days—never saw a person I knew.

DICK: Until the bank.

BUG: *(Laughing.)* Until the bank. I go in—big sunglasses—haven't shaved—wait in line. Go up to a teller—a little blonde number—give her the note.

DICK: And...

BUG: And she looks at the note—and then at me—then at the note again—then at me again...then she says, "Michael?"

DICK: No!

BUG: YA! I didn't say anything—just looked at her real mean-like. She says, "Michael? Michael, it's me. Don't you remember? Irene?"

DICK: Who's Irene?

BUG: Fucked if I know! I said, "It's not Michael—just give me the money."

DICK:     And she said…

BUG:     She said, "Of course it's Michael, we went out in Grade Eleven."

DICK:     No!

BUG:     And I have no fucking idea who she is. And she says, "Listen, do you need some money?"

DICK:     Oh!

BUG:     And then wait—she says, "How's your mom doin'?"

DICK:     AH!

BUG:     AH! I fuckin' ran! *And* she probably fingered me to the cops! Run out of town by Irene!

DICK:     Viva Bandito! *(They laugh.)*

BUG:     Ya, Viva… *(The laugh fades.)*

DICK:     How could you not remember her?

BUG:     I don't remember last year…

DICK:     You are so lucky.

BUG:     Oh ya, I've been blessed.

> *(Beat. Then they laugh again.)*

DICK:     You should stay away from banks.

BUG:     I guess so.

> *(Pause.)*

So how's Donnie doin'.

DICK:     Dead.

BUG:     Aw, no eh?

DICK:     No, you fuckin' freak. We went to his trial, remember? Jesus, get aware of stuff.

BUG:     Ahhhh f—

| | |
|---|---|
| DICK: | They nailed Donnie up and down the street, for the stolen money, the wallets, the car, and for killing Billy, which I'm still pissed off at you for. |
| BUG: | What he get? |
| DICK: | Nine years. He said Billy stole the car. |
| BUG: | Will he talk? |
| DICK: | Donnie? No... He's in heaven. He'll get the best medical treatment known to man—he won't spend a day in a cell, he'll be in the infirmary treated like some grand invalid—getting FREE morphine, all he wants, and organ transplants like a young Frankenstein! Fuck no. He won the lottery. He's probably pissed 'cause he'll have to take parole in 3 or 4 years. |
| BUG: | If he lives that long. |
| DICK: | They'll keep him alive to finish his time. Fuck he'll outlive us all! He'll have all new innards in a few years—and no, he won't talk—Donnie's a good guy—he won't break code. |
| BUG: | That's why I didn't mind doin' that Billy fucker. |
| DICK: | Well...ya, he would've blabbed. |
| BUG: | To anybody! |
| DICK: | Little fucker. |
| | *(Beat.)* |
| BUG: | It was like he wanted me to kill him. |
| DICK: | He was persistent. |
| BUG: | Ya—like he kept buggin' me to—do you think he wanted to die? |
| DICK: | *(Thinks.)* ...I don't think anybody wants to die. Well, most people don't. I think he just wanted to fight you. Like a dog, or like a horse, you know? A young male trying to beat the old stallion, and be the new...whatever. |

BUG:        *(Thinks.)* ...I'm not *that* old.

            *(Beat.)*

DICK:       You fucked that up. That was a perfectly good plan.

BUG:        Oh fuck off.

DICK:       No, shut up—I'm pissed—if we could've just sat
            there—everything had worked perfectly up to that
            point—

BUG:        Perfectly?

DICK:       Yes.

BUG:        Jesus, I've been in on some pretty stupid hits,

DICK:       Yes you have.

BUG:        but you oughta go down in history, as the only
            asshole to ever convince one guy to rob a bank—
            *(Laughing.)* and then another guy to give the fuckin'
            money back!

DICK:       It would've worked

BUG:        You can't base a hit on a bank, on waiting for some
            fuckin' repair guys to show up—

DICK:       They always came right away!

BUG:        It could have been days!

DICK:       I could've waited!

BUG:        Well I couldn't! Not with fucking Charlie Manson
            behind me!

            *(Pause.)*

DICK:       Well...ya can't kill people. I know, we've done a lot
            of bad guys in our time, but—ya can't take someone
            out, just 'cause they piss you off. If you wanted to
            get to him, you should've ignored him.

BUG:        Oh ya, with a knife at my throat.

DICK:       O.K. but ya gotta stop. We gotta stop. 'Cause one of

these times Bugboy—someone's gonna get you…
And I don't want you to die. I know that might
sound…I don't care what it sounds like—we've
spent too much time together to have you go fuck it
up—over nothing.

> *(Beat.)*

And another thing. He wasn't bad looking. No
more killing anybody who looks good. There's
enough ugly motherfuckers on this sad-ass planet
to last forever. Without you going around, picking
off the few that aren't. D'you want everyone to look
like you?

> *(Pause.)*

BUG: Fag.

> *(Beat.)*

DICK: Cocksucker.

BUG: Dogfucker.

DICK: Shit-eating motherfucker.

BUG: *(Thinks.)* …Rimmer.

> *(They laugh.)*

DICK: So aren't you glad I told you to give Donnie the
blade?

BUG: Ya, ya, you're a fucking genius.

DICK: Donnie's glad.

> *(Beat.)*

I'm glad.

BUG: All right, I'm glad, thank you, fuck off.

> *(Beat. DICK moves to the stereo.)*

DICK: I got something for you.

BUG: What are you talking about.

DICK:      *(At the cassette deck, looking for a tape.)* It's nothing. I saw it and I thought, Bug needs this. So I stole it for you.

BUG:       What.

DICK:      *(Finds tape.)* This. *(Throws it to him.)*

           *(Beat.)*

BUG:       This is my *Born To Run*.

DICK:      No, I saw it in a store.

BUG:       This is my tape, I recognize the scratches on the case. Where did you get this?

DICK:      O.K. I didn't get it new, I saw it over at Donnie's place, and I picked it up for you.

BUG:       That little fucker, I *knew* he fuckin' ripped me off, and you wouldn't let me kill him.

DICK:      Now he might have bought the same tape.

BUG:       Why did you defend him?

DICK:      'Cause I needed him, arsewipe, alive. And maybe he didn't steal it. Maybe someone else took it, and left it at his place.

BUG:       Maybe you took it.

           *(Beat.)*

DICK:      Maybe you left it in my machine.

           *(Pause.)*

BUG:       Oh fuck it, put it on, play it... *(Throws him the tape.)*

DICK:      *(As he moves to player.)* So...what are you gonna do now?

BUG:       Same as always...fuck all.
           Where we gonna get tomorrow's stuff?

DICK:      I been saving this. *(Shakes pill bottle.)* Donnie's.

That'll do us a few days. And by then, we'll have lots of money.

BUG:    Ya.

DICK:   You want to know how?

BUG:    How what?

DICK:   How we're gonna get all this money... You want to hear my new thing?

BUG:    What?

DICK:   *(As he turns on power, inserts tape.)* You want to hear my idea, my new plan I been working on.

BUG:    Not in this fuckin' lifetime you pathetic / freak—as if I would ever listen to anything

DICK:   Just hold your fucking horses mister, you're the pathetic fuck who fucked the last one, which was perfect I might add, until you decided that you had to kill someone/ just to pass the time

BUG:    Perfect? Perfect? If *any* of the asshole ideas that you ever came up with, were even close to Possible, do you think that we would've spent the last twenty odd years in / those little rooms with the bars?

DICK:   I already told you, don't blame any of your time on me. If you weren't so stupid, you'd've become a wrestler—

BUG:    OOOHHHH...

DICK:   A wrestler like I told you!

BUG:    *(Laughing.)* Don't even waste your breath.

DICK:   All right, all right, I won't... I'm not.

        *(Beat.)*

        But you want to hear my thing?

BUG:    Play the tape.

DICK:   *(Finger on the button.) Then* you'll listen to it?

BUG:        Play it.

DICK:       Are you sure?…

BUG:        *(Pissed off, says nothing.)*

DICK:       You want another beer before I start?

BUG:        Yes! No!

DICK:       Yes! *(Pushes "Play" button on tape machine.)*

BUG:        Fuck, I never said yes.

DICK:       Yes! / You said yes!

BUG:        Don't start with me!

DICK:       YOU SAID YES.

            Ladies and gentlemen, we have another player.

            > *(Music starts, low, gradually builds. DICK gets two beer from fridge, dances towards the laughing BUG.)*

            O.K. Bugboy, this one involves a car, which you get, and not an old shitbox like you usually find, but a new one, a rich one, one with a phone in it. 'Cause this my boy is a phone scam, yes I said phone. *(Spelling.)* F-O-N-E. And we are gonna make fucking millions, more money than any telethon ever raised for any poor pathetic fuck like you…

            > *(DICK continues to talk, and dance, and sell his plan, as the music rises and drowns him out, and BUG listens, and laughs, and the lights fade to black.)*

            *The End*